Life After Narcissistic Abuse: There Is Healing and Hope

By Cynthia Bailey-Rug

© Copyright 2015 by Cynthia Bailey-Rug. All rights reserved. No part of this publication may be reproduced in any form without written permission by the author. Please visit http://www.CynthiaBaileyRug.com to contact author via her website or email author at CynthiaBaileyRug@aol.com.

Unless otherwise noted, all Scriptures are taken from the King James Version of the Bible.

Scripture quotations from THE MESSAGE. Copyright © by Eugene H. Peterson 1993, 1994, 1995, 1996, 2000, 2001, 2002. Used by permission of Tyndale House Publishers, Inc.

Scripture quotations marked (AMP) are taken from the Amplified Bible, Copyright © 1954, 1958, 1962, 1964, 1965, 1987 by The Lockman Foundation. Used by permission.

ISBN: 978-1-329-35112-7

Dedication:

This book is dedicated to all who have survived narcissistic abuse. May God bless and comfort you as you heal.

Other books by this author:

Non-fiction:

It's All About Me! The Facts About Maternal Narcissism

You Are Not Alone!

Emerging From The Chrysalis

A Witness Of Faith

Lessons From The Heart: What Animals Have Taught Me About Life And Love

All I Know About Marriage...I Learned The Hard Way!

Pawprints On Our Hearts

Baptism Of Joy

Romantic Inspirations

Facets Of Love

Fiction:

Sins Of The Father

The Christian Woman's Guide To Killing Her Husband

Table Of Contents

Introduction i
Chapter One - Describing Narcissistic Personality Disorder 1
Chapter Two - Preparing To Heal 12
Chapter Three - Low Self-Esteem 17
Chapter Four – Shame 23
Chapter Five - You Do Not Know The Real You 27
Chapter Six - Depression 31
Chapter Seven - Anger 36
Chapter Eight - Anger At Those Who Did Not Help 40
Chapter Nine - Blaming God 43
Chapter Ten - Feeling Robbed 46
Chapter Eleven - Bitterness And Negativity 51
Chapter Twelve - Anxiety 54
Chapter Thirteen - Shock 59
Chapter Fourteen - Absolute Thinking 62
Chapter Fifteen - Stifled Creativity 65
Chapter Sixteen - That Vicious Inner Critic 69
Chapter Seventeen - People Pleasing 71
Chapter Eighteen - Always Apologizing 74
Chapter Nineteen - An Overdeveloped Sense Of Responsibility 76
Chapter Twenty - Rejecting Your Femininity 78
Chapter Twenty One - Physical Affection Can Be Difficult 83
Chapter Twenty Two - Being An Introvert 85
Chapter Twenty Three - Dissociation 89
Chapter Twenty Four - Triggers 93
Chapter Twenty Five - Complex Post Traumatic Stress Disorder
.... 97
Chapter Twenty Six - Trauma Changes You 102
Chapter Twenty Seven - Dreams 106
Chapter Twenty Eight - Sickness 110

Chapter Twenty Nine - Bad Days Happen 114
Chapter Thirty - Narcissistic Abuse Changes All Of Your Relationships 116
Chapter Thirty One - You Are The Black Sheep Of Your Family 122
Chapter Thirty Two - Dating Or Marrying A Narcissist 125
Chapter Thirty Three - The Good Things 129
Chapter Thirty Four - What Now? 131
Epilogue 139
Index 141
About The Author 149
Where To Find Cynthia Bailey-Rug Online 151

Introduction

Surviving a relationship with a narcissist is no small accomplishment! Whether that narcissist is a friend, spouse, sibling, or a parent, the pain they can inflict upon their victims and the damage they can do is indescribable, and often lasts a lifetime. Worst of all is the fact that they do not care in the least about what they have done to you. Their lack of caring or even the obvious joy that they show knowing they have hurt you seems to make the pain even worse.

In this book, I hope to help you to heal from and teach you what I have learned about the complicated task of healing from narcissistic abuse.

While many people know and understand Narcissistic Personality Disorder fairly well, they are often oblivious as to what to expect when healing from narcissistic abuse. Very little is said about the healing process compared to Narcissistic Personality Disorder. This leads to a large group of people living with problems that they do not understand. Possibly, they may not even connect their problems to being abused by a narcissist.

To add insult to injury, many people do not understand the incredible amount of pain and suffering that narcissistic abuse entails, and they will make you feel inferior for having problems resulting from it. They do not understand that narcissistic abuse is extremely insidious - it invades every single part of your being. They often think narcissism simply means someone is very selfish, when the reality is it is so much more than that. Narcissistic abuse can destroy your self-esteem and even your sanity, yet many people act as if you, the victim, are overreacting or exaggerating its effects.

If the abusive narcissist in your life is your mother, this brings on a whole new level of invalidating, painful comments, such as:

- "That is your MOTHER! How can you talk about her like that?"
- "She won't be around forever yanno!"
- "She's the only mother you'll ever have and you should treat her better!"
- "You need to make things right with her!"

So many people put all mothers on a pedestal, even the abusive ones. This can be even more difficult for those in the Christian community, because if you say anything less than positive about your mother, no matter how true it is, so many people automatically quote Exodus 20:12 which says, **"Honour thy father and thy mother: that thy days may be long upon the land which the LORD thy God giveth thee." (KJV)** Personally, I find it very interesting that so many of the people who are very quick to quote this Scripture seem to fail to remember Ephesians 6:4, **"Fathers, do not irritate and provoke your children to anger [do not exasperate them to resentment], but rear them [tenderly] in the training and discipline and the counsel and admonition of the Lord." (AMP)** and Colossians 3:21, **"Fathers, do not provoke or irritate or fret your children [do not be hard on them or harass them], lest they become discouraged and sullen and morose and feel inferior and frustrated. [Do not break their spirit.]" (AMP).**

As a result of this dysfunctional thinking about mothers that is so prevalent in society, the victim often feels invalidated, and often wonders if she is overreacting, reading too much into things, being too sensitive or is the reason her mother treats her so poorly. She may end up not discussing her pain, and suffering in silence. This is very wrong!

If you have read any of my writing, then you know I grew up with narcissistic parents, was previously married to a narcissist, and my current husband's parents are also narcissists. I have plenty of unwanted and unasked for experience in the area of Narcissistic Personality Disorder. Probably as much as some mental health professionals, even though I never have worked in the mental health field. I also have no formal education in mental health. However, I became a Christian in 1996, and since then, God has helped me tremendously to heal and to learn about this evil and dangerous disorder. Most recently, God has been teaching me a lot about the recovery process from narcissistic abuse. I have learned that some problems I currently have, have their root in being a victim of narcissistic abuse, even though I never made the connection before. It has been fascinating to me to learn these things since I am intrigued by all things psychological. It also has helped me immensely in my own healing journey.

In this book, my goal is to teach you everything I have learned about healing from narcissistic abuse. Because of my strong faith in God, I will be discussing God a lot, as He has been central to my healing. If you do not share my faith though, please keep reading anyway, as I am sure you still can benefit from what I have learned.

Although everyone's healing is different, we all go through many similar problems. Some problems are hard to connect with narcissistic abuse as they do not seem related at first. I hope covering those problems will give you the answers you are seeking to help you heal.

Healing is not easy, and frankly, I believe it is a lifelong battle, no matter how strong or how weak your faith in God. The abuse is truly all-encompassing. There are many ups and downs, good and bad days. Some days, you are going to be frustrated with the symptoms and problems, and feel like giving up. Such things are all very normal, although you probably will doubt that as you are going through them. You also may lose relationships with people who do not understand what you are going through. However, I want to encourage you to keep on moving forward! Your worst day healing is still much better than your best day being abused by a narcissist!

Because of the fact that most people who contact me are women with narcissistic mothers, I will be writing this book mostly for daughters with narcissistic mothers, from the perspective of a daughter with a narcissistic mother. It also will make writing it a bit easier for me, writing from my own perspective instead of trying to focus on including everyone. Due to the abuse I lived through, I have a lot of trouble with focus and concentration. (Yes, narcissistic abuse can do actual physical damage to your brain. I have what is known as Complex Post Traumatic Stress Disorder which came from years of narcissistic abuse. I will discuss it in more detail in a future chapter.)

That being said, I believe this book will be helpful for anyone, male or female, Christian or not, who has suffered abuse at the hands of someone with Narcissistic Personality Disorder since many narcissists act very similar, and the damage they cause is often also very similar.

Chapter One - Describing Narcissistic Personality Disorder

Since you have purchased this book, it is safe to assume you already know quite a lot about Narcissistic Personality Disorder. However, I would like to explain it in detail in case there are some aspects of it that of which you may not be aware. Knowing as much as you can about Narcissistic Personality Disorder, I believe, is very important in healing from narcissistic abuse. Once you truly understand this disorder, you can see clearly that being abused was not about you or anything you have done. I have found that at some point, most victims blame themselves for "making" their abuser treat them so badly. They think that if they just had been better, kinder, more understanding or more forgiving, she would not have had to treat them so badly. Understanding narcissism is incredibly helpful in finally accepting that what was done to you was not your fault. Narcissists have some really messed up ways of thinking and behaving, which truly have nothing at all to do with you.

Narcissistic Personality Disorder, or NPD, became an actual psychiatric diagnosis in 1968. Prior to that, it was known as megalomania.

I believe Narcissistic Personality Disorder has been around for a very long time prior to receiving the name we know it by today. In fact, the Bible talks about what sounds to me like narcissistic behavior:

2 Timothy 3:1-5
"1 But understand this, that in the last days will come (set in) perilous times of great stress and trouble [hard to deal with and hard to bear].
2 For people will be lovers of self and [utterly] self-centered, lovers of money and aroused by an inordinate [greedy] desire for wealth, proud and arrogant and contemptuous boasters. They will be abusive (blasphemous, scoffing), disobedient to parents, ungrateful, unholy and profane.
3 [They will be] without natural [human] affection (callous and inhuman), relentless (admitting of no truce or appeasement); [they will be] slanderers (false accusers, troublemakers), intemperate and loose in morals and conduct, uncontrolled and fierce, haters of good.
4 [They will be] treacherous [betrayers], rash, [and] inflated with self-conceit. [They will be] lovers of sensual pleasures and vain amusements more than and rather than lovers of God.
5 For [although] they hold a form of piety (true religion), they deny and reject and are strangers to the power of it [their conduct belies the genuineness of their profession]. Avoid [all] such people [turn away from them]." (AMP)

These verses describe a great many people today, sadly, and it describes narcissism very well.

Also, Narcissistic Personality Disorder was named after a character in ancient Greek mythology named Narcissus. Narcissus was an extremely handsome young man. Many loved him, yet he considered no one to be worthy of his love in return. Echo was a beautiful wood nymph who fell in love with Narcissus. Echo however, had a problem. The goddess Hera put a curse on Echo. The once chatty nymph no longer could speak her own words - she could repeat only the last few words she heard.

In the woods one day, Echo saw Narcissus. She wanted to tell him of her passionate love for him, but because of the curse, she was unable to do so. Not understanding what was happening, Narcissus rejected her. Echo retired to the mountains, alone, eventually dying there. This is how the ancient Greeks claimed echoes came into existence.

Narcissus rested by a stream after he rejected Echo. He looked into the water, and when he saw his reflection, he immediately fell in love. Somehow, he did not realize he was only looking at himself! He was so enchanted with his reflection that he refused to leave the place, eventually dying there. A white narcissus flower bloomed there after his death, the only evidence that he was ever in the place.

I find it incredibly accurate that Narcissistic Personality Disorder was named after Narcissus. His extremely selfish behavior is typical of someone with Narcissistic Personality Disorder. They are incredibly, amazingly self-absorbed. Whatever does not directly affect a narcissist directly is unimportant. So you lost your job and have no prospects for a new one on the horizon? That is not important to a narcissist, because it does not directly affect her. You were just diagnosed with a debilitating illness? So what? The narcissist has something much worse than that to live with, and will tell you all about how hard it is for her! Do not bother her with your petty complaints.

There are also two types of narcissists – the overt narcissist and the covert narcissist. Overt narcissists are the "in your face" type. They are loud and proud of their narcissism, often bragging shamelessly about their accomplishments and talents. Covert narcissists are harder to spot. They are much quieter, often feigning innocence, naïveté and helplessness. They appear to be very self-sacrificing, often to the point of martyrdom.

You need to be aware that although Narcissistic Personality Disorder is technically a "disorder," do not believe that means narcissistic people cannot control their hurtful behavior. They absolutely can! Just watch a narcissist around someone they want to impress, and you will see them act a role worthy of an award. Around someone they do not care about impressing, such as a spouse or child? They will be abusive. Narcissistic Personality Disorder is a personality disorder, which makes it different than other mental illnesses. Someone with schizophrenia, for example, has a physical problem with their brain, as does someone with Post Traumatic Stress Disorder or Bipolar Disorder. People with personality disorders do not have physical problems with their brain. They exhibit bad behaviors.

Also, Narcissistic Personality Disorder is known as a spectrum disorder, which means not all narcissists are alike. Some display only a few symptoms of the disorder while others display almost all or even all of them.

Narcissistic mothers fall into two categories – the ignoring narcissistic mother and the engulfing narcissistic mother. The ignoring narcissistic mother cannot be bothered with her child. The child's needs may be met, but grudgingly. The child knows she is not loved by her mother, as her mother does not try to hide that fact. The engulfing narcissistic mother, however, is the polar opposite. She is involved in every single aspect of her child's life. She controls her child completely in the hopes of making that child into whatever it is that she wants her child to be. The child's desires are of no importance whatsoever to the engulfing narcissistic mother, only the mother's desires matter. Many narcissistic mothers swing back and forth between engulfing and ignoring behaviors.

What is at the root of the immeasurably selfish behavior of a narcissist? Why do narcissists act the way they do? Insecurity. Narcissistic people believe deep down, they are horrible people. Most likely, her parent or parents neglected or rejected her as a young child. My mother is a very good example of this. Her own mother was a cruel, heartless woman. She told my mother repeatedly as a child how happy she was when she found out she was pregnant with my aunt, yet a couple of years later she was terribly disappointed she was when she found out she was pregnant with my mother. My mother's sister was the smart one, the pretty one, the successful one, etc. while my mother could not do anything right, and was the "ugly" child. Her mother also left her alone often for long periods of time as a child (her parents separated when she was only six). The last time she saw her father, she was only eight years old, because her mother refused to allow her father to see his children. My grandmother was a textbook case of an ignoring narcissistic mother.

Another possible cause of NPD is parents who spoil their child. Never telling their child no can lead to the child growing up believing that she is entitled to anything and everything she wants. Also, a child who is spoiled does not need to do much for herself because her parents take care of everything. This leaves her insecure, doubting her own abilities. That along with her entitled attitude means she grows into an adult who depends on others to take care of her.

Whatever caused the person's insecurity was so severe, that the person with Narcissistic Personality Disorder somehow decided that she needed to convince everyone she comes into contact with (including herself) that she is the most special, wonderful, popular, gifted, talented and beautiful person ever to walk the earth. In order to do that, the overt narcissist will regale you with stories of her successes, and tell you how many people sing her praises. Or, if she is a covert narcissist, she may appear more humble and simply be sure everyone notices her giving and taking care of other people. She may seem almost martyr-like in her willingness to sacrifice for everyone. She also will feign naïveté in order to get others to do things for her, or to take care of her. Either way, everyone who meets her adores her, according to her, and if someone does not, well, that person has a problem! They are just jealous of her, mean spirited, or have no taste. The person is deeply flawed, and not liking the narcissist is proof of that. After all, narcissists are never wrong. At least according to them.

This terrible insecurity also makes the narcissist very competitive and envious. She simply cannot tolerate someone who is more attractive than her, smarter, more talented or more successful. She will do her level best to knock her "competitor" down a few pegs. She will be extremely critical and judgmental in the hopes of making the competitor feel as bad about herself as the narcissist feels inside. She also will lie about her to others and belittle her accomplishments. To the narcissist, it does not matter if this competitor is a stranger, friend, relative or even her own child. The narcissist's fragile image of being the best must be protected at all costs.

The competitiveness also makes a narcissist a terrible mother in-law, especially if she has a son rather than a daughter. She sees her new daughter in-law as competition for her son's time and affections rather than a lovely new addition to the family. She is highly possessive of her son, demanding much of his time and attention. She will criticize anything and everything about the daughter in-law, and give her plenty of unasked for advice. She has no problems snooping through her daughter in-law's things, even her purse, if she has the inclination. (My mother in-law did this to me until I finally started locking my purse in the trunk of our car when my husband and I were at her house.). The home this woman shares with the narcissist's son? The narcissistic mother in-law claims to be her son's home, and acts as if the daughter in-law is invading that space. If her daughter in-law asks how to make a certain dish that the mother in-law makes, the narcissistic mother in-law will not be flattered as most people would be. Instead, she is angry, because she wants to be the only one who can make that dish. She may flat out refuse to give her daughter in-law the recipe or give it to her, but changing the ingredients around so it turns out poorly when the daughter in-law makes it, claiming it was an innocent mistake. And, the narcissistic mother in-law may tell her new daughter in-law all about how wonderful her son's ex-girlfriend was, and how madly in love with her he was. In fact, she may continue to keep in touch with this woman for years after they broke up, and mention her from time to time. (My husband's mother and sisters have kept in touch with one of my husband's ex-girlfriends since they broke up in the early 1990's.).

People with Narcissistic Personality Disorder are exceptionally touchy about criticism. While it is true no one likes it, it is also true that no one responds to it like a narcissist. When a person is criticized, it may damage their self-esteem. With most people, it can be shaken off quickly, and if the criticism is true, the person either tries to change or decides not to change. With a narcissist, criticism is potentially very threatening to the false image of themselves that they have worked so hard to create. Anything that damages that image is called a narcissistic injury, and when that injury happens, a narcissistic rage is likely to follow. Narcissistic rage can be giving someone the silent treatment, saying spiteful, hurtful things to them, screaming at them or even physically assaulting them. Often, the type of narcissistic rage changes as the narcissist ages. I have seen this with my mother. When I was a child, she calmly said horrid, hurtful things when we were alone. In my mid to late teen years, she began screaming viciously at me when we were alone or would refuse to speak to me for a short time. Since I moved out of her home at nineteen, she has given me lengthy silent treatments more times than I can count, has told my in-laws how horrible I am, once threatened to contact a former landlord because I had more cats than the lease allowed simply because I disagreed with something she said, and continued to use the scathing criticisms. Now that she is in her mid-seventies, my mother's favorite way to let loose her narcissistic rage is either to give me the silent treatment or quietly to say incredibly hurtful, cruel things to me in a public place knowing I will not create a scene. Or, if I do, she will be thrilled because I will look like a crazy, evil daughter being so cruel to her innocent elderly mother.

People with Narcissistic Personality Disorder have absolutely no empathy. They are absolutely unwilling to put themselves in another person's position and understand their pain. So long as that pain does not directly affect the narcissist, it means absolutely nothing to her. If you have a problem, and try to discuss it with a narcissist, you are going to be hurt and invalidated. She will tell you how much harder she had it than you, how much more severe her pain is than yours, or how she would not have let that happen to her. She also may simply ignore whatever you said, and turn the conversation back to her. In any case, your pain will be invalidated.

Narcissistic people also are extremely entitled. Since they have convinced themselves that they are special, then by golly this means they are entitled to anything and everything they want! Your needs and wants however? They do not matter. Hers are much more important than yours ever could be.

This entitlement attitude also makes the narcissist demanding. If you are dealing with a demanding narcissist, you have to have and stringently enforce healthy boundaries. If you do not, you will be used until you have nothing left to give, and she still will put demands on you.

Interestingly, in spite of being very demanding and entitled, narcissists are cowards at heart. Certainly, they do not come across that way when screaming at you to do something for them, but they are. Narcissists are bullies. They are simply putting on a good show to make themselves look big and bad, but inside they are hoping you will not see that this is just an act on their part. This bully mentality is also why narcissists have more courage online, in text messages or on the telephone than in person. It is easier for them to be brave when they can hide behind a computer or telephone.

Narcissists do not care to learn and grow. Most people have the ability to look at themselves, and change things they do not like. They also adapt their behaviors if they learn something is hurting another person, or simply not working for them for whatever reason.

Narcissists however, have absolutely no interest in such things. The narcissist at age twenty-five will be the same person when she reaches seventy-five. Only minor changes will occur, such as I mentioned with the narcissistic rage changing as the narcissist ages.

Rather than deal appropriately with her flaws, the narcissist prefers to project them onto other people, in particular her child. This projection means she accuses her child of doing things that the child is not doing, but she is. For example, my mother has insulted my weight for my entire life. I was not a fat child, but according to her, I was "broad across the beam," which was her way of saying my backside was too big. Her constant criticism was so bad, I went through anorexia (about the time I was ten) and bulimia (in my teenage years). Yet interestingly, my mother has been significantly overweight most of her life. Even now that she is thinner, she still carries a lot of extra weight, and I at my heaviest have never weighed as much as she does.

The narcissistic mother will put her fears and insecurities on her child as well as her flaws. If she has a fear of water, for example, she will tell her child that she does not understand what is wrong with people who like to swim. Do they not know they are going to drown? She will say this and similar things over and over until the child develops a fear of water as well, even if the child never has been swimming.

Narcissists are extremely skilled at reading people. It seems odd since they are so self absorbed, does it not? Yet it is true. This people reading skill enables them to know who they can abuse and what tactics they can use that will be the most successful.

They are also extremely hypocritical. If a narcissist does something bad, that is fine, but if you do the exact same thing, you are a terrible person. My mother says she cannot stand someone who brags about themselves, yet if you are alone with her for any length of time, she will entertain you with stories of her many successes in life.

Narcissistic parents use their children in many ways, but possibly the most harmful for the child is when they treat their child more like a romantic partner than their child. They confide in their child about their marriage problems, their sex life and other inappropriate intimate details that should be shared only with their partner or very close friends. It often looks to other people as though the parent and child are simply close. Many people may think it is a good thing, but it is not. This is called emotional incest. It may or may not include actual sexual contact. Either way, emotional incest (also known as covert incest, parentalizing or parentification) causes a great deal of psychological harm to the child.

Narcissists have no boundaries in any area at all. Your "yes" and "no" mean absolutely nothing to a narcissist, especially as a child. If you are her child, she will barge into your bedroom or bathroom at any time she wants, whether your door is open or closed. She may snoop through your things or give away your belongings. After all, she believes her child to be an extension of her, something she may use however she wants, so why would such a person have any right to any boundaries?

Speaking of a lack of boundaries, many narcissists also like to show off their bodies. They wear inappropriately skimpy clothing (or even no clothing around the house) or act in a sexually inappropriate way. A narcissistic mother may flirt with or try to steal her daughter's boyfriend, even if that daughter is a teenager. Some narcissistic mothers are exactly the opposite, and are very prudish. They tell their children sex is dirty, disgusting, an awful sacrifice a woman must endure in order to have a baby.

Narcissists live for attention. It does not matter if the attention is positive or negative, so long as they get it. Some will use that inappropriate sexual behavior to get attention while others may use bizarre behavior. There is no low too low for a narcissist to go to get the attention they crave. I remember once having lunch in a restaurant with my parents. My father and I started talking, and inadvertently left my mother out of the conversation. She picked up a napkin, and pretended to blow her nose, making disgusting "ppffftttt" noises with her mouth. People in nearby booths looked our way. When my father and I looked at her in shock, she pulled the napkin away, and laughed a very disturbing, deranged laugh. This episode scared me, as it showed me just how unstable and how narcissistic my mother truly is.

Narcissists are good at mirroring other people's behavior in order to lure them into their web. People naturally are more comfortable with those who share their interests and who act much like they do. Narcissists know this, and will do this if it means they can use a new victim. They also may do it after they realize they have upset you in order to get back in your good graces.

They also have a complete arsenal of weapons at their disposal designed to get them whatever results they want. No, they may not necessarily have a gun or knife, but they have weapons nonetheless. Narcissists are excellent manipulators. They will criticize, use guilt trips, intimidate, distort your reality, make you doubt your sanity (gaslighting/crazymaking), lie, make themselves look like the victim instead of you, and anything else they can do to get their way.

Most of the weapons of a narcissist are extremely subtle, such as giving dirty looks that others cannot see, tone of voice or body language. The subtlety is partly what makes narcissistic abuse so hard to explain to those who are unfamiliar with it, I think. Saying something like, "My mother gave me a dirty look" really does not sound so bad. However, to those of us familiar with what it is like to have a narcissistic mother, we realize that the "dirty look" can be a predecessor to a vicious narcissistic rage. It can mean that we have disappointed or angered our mother yet again, and that she will spew a long list of criticisms designed to devastate the self-esteem.

Chapter Two - Preparing To Heal

While I covered a great deal about the things that can happen as a result of years of narcissistic abuse in my last book, "It's All About ME! The Facts About Maternal Narcissism," once the book was published, for the first time, I began to see other problems I had that were directly connected to the narcissistic abuse I have experienced. I do not know of any area in my life that was not somehow affected by being abused by narcissists. In fact, when I was seventeen, I learned my mother even affected my voice! I had gotten myself into counseling, and on one of our first visits, the counselor pointed out something very interesting. I was extremely soft-spoken back then, barely speaking over a whisper. She mentioned this to me, and suggested that I was so soft-spoken because I was trying to quiet down my much louder mother. In my heart, I knew she was right, and promptly began to find my own voice. Being soft-spoken never quieted my mother anyway, so it was not accomplishing the desired results. I am still a bit soft spoken today, but nothing like I was as a child.

Narcissistic abuse is insidious and evil, and it truly permeates every fiber of your being. Recovery is so incredibly difficult because of this. It feels like you constantly are seeing another area that was affected, and you have to work on healing. Exasperating does not begin to describe this feeling!

The good news however is that you can heal from narcissistic abuse. Much of the abuse has skewed how you think, and dysfunctional thinking patterns can be changed into healthy ones, thank God!

Other damage may be more permanent, such as in cases of being physically assaulted or if you have Complex Post Traumatic Stress Disorder. C-PTSD is very common among survivors of narcissistic abuse. I have had many of the symptoms most of my life. It manifested fully in 2012. I am still learning new ways to live with the annoying symptoms.

As I mentioned in the introduction, we are going to focus in this book on learning what problems you have that are connected to narcissistic abuse and how to heal from or at least manage them. I do believe healing to be a lifelong battle, but please do not be discouraged. You do not need to be totally healed before you will be happier and more peaceful. Even small steps will help those things to happen.

As you work on your healing, you need to be willing to take breaks often. It is a common thing for those who first learn about narcissism to become obsessed. I was the same way. I thought, finally! There was an answer to what I had experienced, and surprisingly, I was not to blame like everyone said I was! It was so exciting, I had to learn more. And more. And still more. I read anything and everything possible about Narcissistic Personality Disorder. Then I started writing about it in my blog and later writing books. It felt like all I thought about was narcissism. I was depressed and then the Complex Post Traumatic Stress Disorder manifested in full force. That was when I finally realized this was no good. Yes, it is good and wise to learn about narcissism and healing from narcissistic abuse, but it is equally good and wise to take breaks from it often. Narcissistic Personality Disorder and narcissistic abuse are very deep, intense subjects. They require a lot of energy and focus to understand, and learning about them really can be an emotional roller coaster.

The brain is like the body in that sometimes it can work too hard, and needs to rest. Learning about narcissism and ways to heal from its abuse is very hard work. You will need to give your brain that rest it needs periodically by taking time as you feel you need it to focus on anything but narcissism and your healing. During those times, deliberately refuse to think about those topics, and focus on lighter things, such as hobbies you enjoy. Do things that bring you joy during those times.

Do not judge yourself as you heal. Healing is a very different experience for everyone. Do not berate yourself if you are not healing as fast as someone else you know who also experienced narcissistic abuse. People are extremely different in every way. What affected you deeply and is taking you a while to heal from may not have affected your friend at all, or vice versa. That does not make one of you wrong and the other right, it only makes you different, and different does not mean wrong or bad.

Accept the fact that you are going to go backwards sometimes. Yes, it is unpleasant to experience, but it is also normal. Healing from anything is never a straight path, but more like a twisty, winding mountain road with a few big ditches along the way. Use those backsliding moments as learning experiences rather than beating yourself up over them.

As you start to heal, naturally you will want to discuss your experiences. This is going to feel very awkward for you at first. Narcissists love secrecy and isolation, as both allow them to do as they see fit without fear of anyone stopping them. Narcissistic parents in particular over narcissistic spouses, friends, etc. seem to have a knack for enforcing silence of all members of the household without actually saying the words, "I don't want you to tell anyone what I do to you." You somehow understand discussing their actions will not end well for you, so you grow up keeping everything secret. When you finally do start discussing what you have gone through, it will feel very foreign at first since you have not done it before. You also may feel guilty for being disloyal to the family unit by breaking the silence. Fear may be a part of the equation as well, because you are expecting a narcissistic rage if your actions are discovered. All of these feelings are totally normal. They do diminish over time, although I am unsure if they ever go away completely. I have been writing about narcissism for about three years to date, and in all honesty, sometimes I still worry that my parents might find out what I write about. I guess one kind of good thing about them both being narcissistic is that neither has any interest in what I write, so they rarely ask me about my writing.

Always remember that people have very strong feelings about narcissistic abuse. Those who have been through it most likely will understand your struggles. Some may not though if your struggles and theirs are quite different. They may try to convince you to do what worked for them, even though you know it will not work for you. Do not let them persuade you to do something that you do not feel is right for you! You know best what you need to do for yourself, especially if you trust God to guide you.

Others who have not experienced narcissistic abuse probably will not understand what you are going through. They may judge you, criticize you or trivialize your experiences and invalidate your pain. Sadly, this is a very common phenomenon, especially when the narcissistic abuser is a parent, and in particular, a mother. So many people cannot comprehend a parent abusing their own child, and they make excuses for the abusive parent. This is extremely hurtful and frustrating! In the early days of your healing, it can make you feel guilty for talking about these things, wonder if you are exaggerating, or even crazy. These are completely normal ways to feel in that situation.

Just do your best to remember what happened to you - it was horrible abuse. You are not exaggerating or crazy for being affected by it! You are a normal human being who survived abnormal circumstances!

I have found writing to be immensely helpful in my healing journey. Not only writing my books and blog, but writing in my personal journal. There is something extremely validating about seeing your experiences in writing. It also comes in very handy when either dealing with someone who invalidates what you have been through or dealing with the narcissist to have things written down. You have a written record of things to refer back to for those times you are doubting your experiences and feelings. It helps you to keep a good perspective on things as well as to reassure you that yes, those things did happen that way, and yes, they were extremely painful.

As you begin to focus on healing from narcissistic abuse, you are going to feel very selfish, because you are thinking about yourself for the first time. It feels so foreign to think of yourself when you have spent so much time thinking only of others, especially your narcissistic mother. However, it is necessary to think of yourself! Every healthy person has some degree of narcissism. It is what enables a person to say no to doing something that goes against their personal beliefs or endangers them. That is healthy. Narcissists take a good thing too far, but since you understand narcissism, you are not going to do that. Knowing a narcissist can make you a bit paranoid of becoming like them, which is not necessarily a bad thing.

Chapter Three - Low Self-Esteem

Among the most common problems associated with recovering from narcissistic abuse is low self-esteem.

The constant gaslighting done by narcissists can take a drastic toll on anyone's self-esteem. How could it not? When someone constantly tells you the things you see, feel, believe and do are not only completely wrong, but there is something deeply wrong with you for seeing, feeling, believing and doing those things, naturally you are going to feel deeply flawed, wrong, bad or even crazy.

Being abused by a narcissist and not being allowed to have your own needs, wants or feelings also leads to low self-esteem. The reason is because you end up feeling as if your only purpose is to serve the narcissist. You feel much like a tool - as if you are something to be taken out, used as needed, then put back on a shelf or in a drawer when you are no longer needed.

The lack of empathetic behavior narcissists display constantly also leads to low self-esteem in their victims, because they make certain you know that your problems mean absolutely nothing to them. Their problems are much more important. So are the problems of anyone and everyone else other than you. This is especially true in cases of a narcissistic mother. Mothers are the most important person in a child's early life, god-like, really. If she, this incredibly important person in your life, shows you that the problems that are so important to you really are not important at all to her, this naturally makes you feel as if something is wrong with you for feeling the way you do.

The indescribably selfish behavior of someone with Narcissistic Personality Disorder also can contribute to low self-esteem. Narcissistic mothers act as if their child does not even have wants, needs, feelings or thoughts, only the narcissistic mother has these things according to her. Or, if the child presents them to her mother, the narcissistic mother clearly does not want to be bothered with them. As a result, this child grows up feeling as if she basically needs to be invisible. Never bother anyone, especially the narcissistic mother, with such trivial things. Never be a burden. Never bother anyone with those wants, needs, thoughts or feelings because they are so unimportant. Important people, like the narcissistic mother, are the only ones allowed to have needs, feelings and thoughts. Feeling invisible is so frustrating and painful. I know, as I have battled this for my entire life. It has only been recently I have been able to describe what I was feeling and learn why I felt that way.

Narcissists act as if they are superior to everyone else, which makes others in their company feel as though they truly are inferior to the narcissist, and devastates self-esteem over time. Over time, this air of superiority they possess can make you feel as if you do not deserve things. What things? Anything, even basic things such as respect and politeness. Narcissists think are so much more important than you, and will never hesitate to let you know exactly how unimportant you really are.

And of course, narcissists love to viciously criticize other people in order to build themselves up. Most people build themselves up in a much healthier way, such as listening to complements or acknowledging their own accomplishments, but narcissists prefer to tear down others instead. I heard a story many years ago that reminds me of this. A farmer's old mule fell down a hole in the ground. He could not get the mule out, so he decided to let the mule die in the hole. Daily, he threw trash down the hole, and daily the mule stomped down the trash. One day, the trash was piled so high under the mule's feet, he was able to walk out of the hole. While the moral of the story was to inspire you to use the bad things for good in your life, it also reminds me of how someone with Narcissistic Personality Disorder gains their self-esteem. They have to stomp down someone (like that mule stomped down the trash) until they are raised up.

Thankfully, it is very possible to regain the self-esteem that the narcissist stole from you. It will take some effort on your part, but it can be done.

Personally I started with studying what God has to say about His children. If God says something, I believe it, and that includes the things He says about His children. As someone who has accepted Jesus as their personal Lord and Savior, you are pretty special to God! He claims you as His child (Acts 1:28). He has chosen you (Ephesians 1:11-12) and you are not a mistake and you have a purpose (Psalm 136:15-16) even if someone may have told you to the contrary! God's own hand created you in your mother's womb, and He made you wonderfully (Psalm 139:13-14). God loves you simply because He is your father and you are His child (1 John 3:1).

There are so many more wonderful Scriptures in the Bible describing God's great love for you. I encourage you to study this topic thoroughly, and write out all of the Scriptures you find on the topic.

Also, listen to the good things people have said about you. Most people are not overly generous with complements, so if they say something good about you, it must be pretty exceptional if they felt the need to mention it.

Look at the things you have accomplished in your life. Have you excelled at your career? Do you have a happy marriage to someone you can describe honestly as your best friend? Have you raised happy, well-adjusted children? Have you followed a dream and accomplished something very special in spite of the nay sayers in your life? These are not easy tasks and you should be very proud of yourself for accomplishing them! You, Dear Reader, are a success!

Also, keep your expectations of yourself realistic. You are going to make mistakes from time to time. Everybody makes mistakes. There is no need to beat yourself up for them. Instead, try thinking of those mistakes as learning experiences, and move on.

Think about what you are thinking about. Do you automatically criticize yourself when you look at yourself in the mirror, picking apart all of your flaws (that most likely are imaginary, by the way!)? When presented with a challenge, do you automatically tell yourself you are not smart enough to do the task? Do you assume you are going to fail? If you do, it is time to start to challenge these thoughts. Is there real evidence you are unable to do the task you need to? Or, are you replaying the messages of narcissistic abuse that tell you what a complete failure the abuser thinks you are? If you are unsure, ask God to help you to learn what the truth is.

Stop assuming those horrible things said about you were right. They are not right! They were said by someone whose only goal was to make you feel as badly about yourself as she feels about herself. What she said was not designed to help you at all, but to hurt you and make herself feel better. Why would you allow someone that cruel and dysfunctional to determine your self-esteem?

Stop comparing yourself to others! I cannot stress this enough. That never goes well. Ever. For anybody. God has created you to be a unique entity. No two people are exactly alike. Everyone is very different. I think God did this so people would need each other rather than being completely self-sufficient. So what if your friend is an executive with her company while you are "only" a secretary? That does not make her better than you. Your co-worker grows a fantastic vegetable garden each summer while you have killed off every house plant you have owned, including the cactus? Who cares? Neither that co-worker nor your friend can create a wonderful, peaceful landscape painting like you can. Your talents are different than other people's talents. Your calling in life is different than other people's callings. That does not make yours inferior, only different.

Always remember too that one constant in life is change. As you age, not only does your body change, but your mind changes too. Something you could do well at age eighteen may be something you no longer can do at forty-eight. It is totally normal, and nothing to fret over.

Another good thing you can do for yourself is to treat yourself. Buy yourself gifts just because. Start out small, perhaps a new bottle of nail polish or a new shirt. You can build up to larger gifts from there if you like, without creating debt you cannot afford, obviously. Giving yourself little gifts raises your spirits. It helps you to feel worthy, and thus raises your self-esteem.

I think a part of having low self-esteem after narcissistic abuse is feeling invisible. You just want to stay out of everyone's way, and make no trouble. Deep down, you believe you are here to do for others, then be ignored when you are not needed, exactly as your narcissistic abuser trained you. This is a horrible way to feel. It hurts when other people treat you this way too. I cannot count how many times I have been on the phone with my narcissistic parents, they have said something very upsetting, I have cried, and they did not even notice I was crying. Granted, I was not loudly sobbing, but at least my suddenly shaky voice should have been a clue to them something was very wrong with me. Since it was not, and my pain was ignored yet again, it hurt me badly.

When you feel invisible, other people often pick up on that and treat you accordingly. For that to stop happening, you need to stop feeling invisible! Improving your self-esteem definitely helps. Also, start to embrace your wants, needs, feelings, and thoughts. You have absolutely every right to have them, just like anyone else, and you need to be fully aware of this fact.

You also need to learn that it is perfectly ok to ask for things from other people sometimes. You have the right to expect certain things from certain people in your life. If you are laid up with a broken leg, there is nothing wrong with expecting your husband and children to take over housework and cooking chores until you are better. It will not kill them, even if they act like it may.

Also work on setting and enforcing some healthy boundaries. You have every right to say no, that is not acceptable sometimes. It not only helps your self-esteem to have healthy boundaries, but it helps your relationships. They become more clearly defined when good boundaries are in place. This offers plenty of freedom and relaxation when both parties in a relationship understand each other's boundaries.

Chapter Four – Shame

Another aspect of low self-esteem is shame. Shame goes beyond feeling badly about yourself. Shame says there is something deeply, inherently wrong with you.

Most people, even ones with healthy self-esteem have felt shame at some point in their lives. If you have cheated on your spouse, you feel shame, because what you did was a very bad thing. This is healthy shame, feeling ashamed of doing something bad.

Unhealthy or toxic shame in that same situation says that you are a horrible person for what you did, instead of saying that you did a horrible thing.

Do you see the difference?

Toxic shame is very common in those who were raised by narcissistic parents. Emotional neglect, constant criticisms and abandonment (either physical or emotional) easily can create toxic shame in children, which will be carried into adulthood.

Toxic shame also manifests in a variety of ways, none of which are good. Last February when I got Carbon Monoxide Poisoning, I did not want my husband to call 911. I did not want to rack up expensive medical bills, and that was more of a priority to me than my own health. I came very close to dying that day, and yet even so I still thought money was more important than my life! I also did not expect the staff in the emergency room to help me in spite of the fact that it is the job of nurses and doctors, to help people. Knowing this, somehow I was still shocked if anyone was nice or helpful to me.

If you think about it though, this behavior of mine makes sense. Toxic shame means you are ashamed of everything about you. You think you are a terrible person, unworthy of anything. Of course money was more important than my health. No wonder I was surprised people were helping me at the hospital, since I believed myself unworthy of any attention or care.

Toxic shame also can make it very hard or even impossible to ask for help. That day in February, I was not calling my husband for help. I only called to complain about not being able to clear out the smoke from the fireplace in the house and the blood all over the floor (Carbon Monoxide Poisoning really messes with your brain due to the lack of oxygen it is getting. I was unaware that these things were bad and a sign of something very wrong at the time.) Even smaller things can be difficult to deal with for someone experiencing toxic shame. Asking my husband for money to put gas in my car or if I can get new clothes can be problematic for me. If money is tight, it is even worse. This is because deep down, I feel I should not be a burden in any way. I should not burden my husband with my problems, even when they are worth discussing or my needs, even when they are very valid.

Does any of this resonate for you as well? Do you have trouble asking for help or feeling unworthy? If so, there is hope! You do not have to live this way!

To be honest, I still am battling toxic shame, but I am winning the battle. I will share with you what has been helping me.

I am trying to be more open with what is going on in my mind. I always hid most of my problems from my husband, especially about the Complex Post Traumatic Stress Disorder. His job can be really stressful, as can his relationship with his narcissistic parents, so I never felt I should "burden" him with my problems. Plus, C-PTSD is a very complex, hard to handle disorder not only for the person with it, but for anyone in a relationship with that person. He has no idea just how complex it is, and it can be frustrating for me trying to make him understand this disorder is not me being too negative or any other simple thing, that it is real brain damage. Rather than try to make him understand, I gave that up and simply stopped discussing it with him. Not any longer. It is not easy since I am so accustomed to keeping things inside, but I have felt God pushing me to be more open. Not only open with my husband, but also in other relationships and with my writing. In all honesty, it is pretty scary and very awkward since I am so very unaccustomed to it, but it is helpful.

Bringing things out into the open helps them to lose their power. Did you ever read any of the old vampire legends from hundreds of years ago? They said that vampires were mighty and powerful in the darkness, yet would turn to dust in the light. Problems can be that way as well. When they are kept inside, they can be overwhelming. Bringing them into the open can put them in a better, healthier perspective. And, talking about these things can make them seem more real somehow, which validates your pain, hurt or frustration with the problem. Validated emotions lessen toxic shame.

Step outside of your comfort zone. I am not saying go cliff diving or anything so drastic, of course. Just push yourself a little bit as you are able to do so. I started by telling some people about my experiences with the Carbon Monxoide Poisoning. Not an easy thing since I was so embarrassed about it at first. I also have been talking more to my husband as I mentioned previously. Doing little things like that which I once would not have done have helped me quite a bit. I think showing yourself you can do things that "normal" people do can be very helpful in reducing toxic shame. These things make you feel more normal, and less like a horrible, freak of a human being.

Address your shaming beliefs. When you feel that toxic shame rearing its ugly head, ask yourself why you feel this way? If you are unsure, ask God for His input. When I got the Carbon Monoxide Poisoning, I asked myself why was I so ashamed of getting sick? I did nothing wrong - it happened due to a problem with my fireplace flue that neither my husband nor I knew was there. No one was to blame. So why the shame? God showed me that it stemmed from my upbringing. My mother has said more times than I can count how hard it was on her when I was sick or injured as a kid. She still laments about how in 1986 when I was fifteen years old, she had to sacrifice her Mother's Day taking care me because I was on crutches and my father who was laid up with a bad back injury. Things like that instilled shame in me for getting sick or hurt, even when neither was my fault. I quickly realized how ridiculous this is. Clearly those were her issues, not mine.

If God would help me so much to heal, certainly He will do the same for you! Let Him help you to heal from toxic shame! Living with it is no way to live. Pray to God often, and follow His promptings on what will help you to heal. You will not be disappointed.

Chapter Five - You Do Not Know The Real You

Being raised by a narcissist, your parents never allowed you to be the person that God made you to be. Instead, your purpose was to be an extension of your narcissistic parent, being what the parent wanted you to be. You were allowed only to look and act the way she wanted you to, not how you really wanted to look or act. The same goes if you have been romantically involved with a narcissist. You were only allowed to look how she wanted you to look and act however she wanted you to act. Living with a narcissist, you certainly are not allowed to have your own interests, either, unless the narcissist approves of them.

This incredibly controlling behavior can leave you feeling lost once you get away from the narcissistic abuse. Not only do you not know who you are or what you like, but now no one is telling you who you are or what you like. So now what do you do?!

You need to get to know the real you, and also to enjoy being that person. Now is the time.

I realize that this can sound like a daunting and very unpleasant task since your self-esteem has been so badly damaged by narcissistic abuse, but truly that is not the case. Once you start to learn who you are, learn your likes and dislikes, you are going to enjoy yourself. This part of healing truly can be a lot of fun! I have thoroughly enjoyed it myself, which was a big surprise to me.

A really good place to start is to take a personality test. The Briggs Myers test is amazing. It is based on Carl Jung's and Isabel Briggs Myers' approach to personality. The results will be a four letter description of your personality. For example, my personality type is the INFJ – Introverted, iNtuitive, Feeling, Judging. INFJ is also the rarest personality type, encompassing about one percent of the entire population, which I think is pretty interesting. I wish I had known about my personality type sooner! I took this test only a few weeks ago and have learned so much since then. Studying my personality type has answered so many questions I once had about myself. It taught me that I am not weird like people told me that I was, but instead, I am a typical INFJ. It was very validating for me to learn this piece of information. My narcissistic mother always has said there is something wrong with me, and my ex husband implied there was something wrong with me. It turns out that there is not, we are simply very different personality types, and learning this has helped me to feel better about myself.

I would like to encourage you to take this test too (it is available for free online), and then research your personality type. I am certain it will benefit you greatly. It will explain why you are the way you are, and show you that you are OK.

Another great way to get to know who you are is to question how you really feel about things. Do you truly like or dislike something for yourself, or have you been told that is how you feel about it? When I was growing up, my mother said she did not like hard rock or heavy metal music, and it was implied I did not either. I assumed I did not, until I heard the music my favorite cousin listens to. He has been a devoted Black Sabbath fan his whole life, and thanks to him, I am too. In fact, he is an avid hard rock/heavy metal fan, and we share a lot of similar music likes. Until I listened to it, I honestly thought I was not a heavy metal fan. For way too long, I blindly believed what my mother said rather than forming my own opinion, and missed out on listening to some music I really enjoy.

You truly need to question things that you feel so you can learn what is truly you, and what was instilled in you by your narcissistic mother. Try things you believe that you do not like to see if you actually do not like them. Also do the same with the things you do like. Ask yourself, do you truly like or dislike those things? If so, great. If not though, why do you force yourself to feel the way you do instead of respecting how you truly feel?

Step outside of your comfort zone and try new things. I know, this is not easy. Going through narcissistic abuse can create so much anxiety in you that your comfort zone becomes a very tiny little place. However, if you can gently force yourself outside your comfort zone as you feel able to do so, it will help you. Try going to different places to see if you like them. Never been to a museum? Go to one and see what you think of it. Did not like the natural history museum? Try an art or science one instead. Read a book in a different genre or listen to music of a different genre.

Try things you have always wanted to try, but did not have the nerve to try. I am not necessarily suggesting sky diving or base jumping (unless that is something you are up for), but try some small things. Or, at least try things you once enjoyed but gave up because your narcissistic mother did not approve of it. In my case, I started to draw again. I did it when I was a kid, but gave up on it. In the last couple of months, I began to draw again, and am getting better at it. I also got some watercolor pencils to use with the drawings. I also tried working with clay and felting. I learned I am not particularly good with either, but that is fine. At least I tried, and learned what I am good and not good at without someone else telling me their opinion of these things.

Also try dressing differently. Only wear clothes that you genuinely like. It may sound like a silly little thing, but it really does make you feel more comfortable and peaceful to dress the way you want to rather than how someone else thinks you should dress. I grew up with my mother dictating how I dressed, then I married my ex husband who wanted me to dress a certain way to please him. I hated the way both of them wanted me to dress. It has taken me years to develop my own style, but I am finally happy with how I dress. And interestingly, my mother often complements what I am wearing! Not that I am out for her approval. I just think it is funny that it turns out she actually does like my style after years of rejecting what I liked and trying to make me wear her style.

Chapter Six - Depression

Depression is a very normal response to narcissistic abuse. Who would not be depressed after constantly being told what a terrible person they are, how selfish, stupid, lazy, ugly, fat, worthless, etc. they are? Whether those words are actually said or simply implied makes no difference to how they feel. They hurt. Plus, if they are implied rather than said directly, there is the crazymaking/gaslighting element that can make you feel crazy, oversensitive or paranoid. This too is extremely depressing.

Even getting away from the narcissist in your life does not mean the depression automatically lifts. It can linger for quite some time even after this person is out of your life. Ending any relationship, even a toxic one, can cause depression for various reasons. You may be questioning whether or not you did the right thing, or wondering if you should give this person another chance. You may wonder if you went too far. Plus, you will think about any good times you had, which will make you miss that person. If the narcissist in question is your parent, you can guarantee these concerns will haunt you even more. It is hard enough deciding to end a relationship with a friend or romantic partner. Ending it with a parent is so much more difficult.

There are many symptoms of depression, such as:

- Feeling hopeless.
- A negative outlook on life.
- Feeling extremely sad.
- Suicidal thoughts.
- Feeling guilty.
- Feeling worthless.
- Irritability.
- Sleep problems (either not being able to sleep or sleeping too much.)
- Constant fatigue.
- Lack of energy.
- Weight loss or gain, often due to the desire to get comfort from food or not wanting to eat.
- Digestive issues.
- Aches and pains without a physical cause.
- Difficulty concentrating.
- Lack of interest in things you once cared deeply about, such as hobbies or sex.

Experiencing these symptoms for a while after something traumatic is perfectly normal. If you lose a loved one, for example, you are going to feel this way for a while, months or even a year or so. However, if you feel this way yet have not recently experienced a traumatic event, something may be wrong. And, if you are thinking about suicide, then please do NOT hesitate to call the National Suicide Prevention Hotline and get some help! They are there to help people in your position. Their number is 1-800-273- TALK (8255)

It is possible for victims of child abuse to live with these symptoms and not realize it. I did exactly that. I had lived depressed and suicidal for so long, I honestly thought it was normal.

The good news is that depression can be managed. I say managed because it never will completely vanish. Even if you are a happy person, there will be times in life where you get depressed, such as when you lose a loved one, the job you love lets you go or other sad things happen. Many things can cause depression, sometimes even things you never thought could do that, such as moving or having surgery. Oddly, even a good change can sometimes cause depression for a short time.

To start with, you need God. He is well able to handle anything you have to say, so let all your feelings out to Him. He will listen and comfort you. He also can help to change your perspective. If you are looking at things too pessimistically, He can help you to see the good in the situation.

Talk it out. Talking to someone caring, non-judgmental and supportive can do wonders for your mood. Knowing someone truly cares can help to alleviate depression.

Sometimes you may not feel up to talking about it. Or, you may feel unable to put what is going on into words. Instead of talking, try writing things out. Journaling is a very valuable tool. Once you start to write, the words may flow, getting your feelings out. Also, as I have said many times, seeing what you have experienced in writing can be very validating. It can show you how strong you are when you see what you have been through in writing. It gives you clarity, too. Sometimes seeing something written down can help you to find a solution when you could not find one before.

Music is a wonderful anti-depressant. What kind of music do you like? Put it on your stereo and crank it up! I love old music from the 1980's that I grew up with. Listening to it always improves my mood. It is funny, because I do not like remembering much of my childhood, but the music from that era still brightens my mood.

Christian music may help you to feel close to God. Native American Indian music is very serene and calming, particularly the pan flute music, as is some Celtic music, New Age, Classical and Opera.

Open your Bible and start reading. Often, this can improve your mood. I find the stories in Genesis fascinating, and the epistles of Paul in the New Testament particularly uplifting.

If you do not feel like reading, then maybe you would do better watching a preacher on television or listening to one on the radio. If you are especially depressed, I would advise finding someone who is preaching on the love of God or another uplifting topic. This is not the time to listen to preaching on the Great Tribulation or other deeper matters.

Be good to yourself, and do it often. Nice little things that make you feel good will help to alleviate depression. Have your favorite herbal teas or coffees readily available, and indulge in them often. Go for a walk in the woods or on the beach. Tinker in your garden. Snuggle your pets. Take bubble baths. Take a day off to lay in bed, watching fun movies.

Get creative. Something about expressing one's creativity can be extremely uplifting.

Indulge your feminine or masculine side often. Ladies, create a beauty ritual that is easy for you to stick to. The ritual need not be elaborate or time consuming if you do not want it to be. Baby your hair, skin and nails. Exfoliate and moisturize your skin often. Get regular manicures and pedicures. Treat your hair gently, as if it was vintage lace. Keep your style easy to maintain. As for you gentlemen, be sure to let your lady pamper you sometimes. Believe it or not, pampering also nurtures your masculinity. Go make something. Use that logical mind of yours to create something interesting. Whether it is building a model airplane or a coffee table, making something will help your mood to improve.

Medications can help to manage depression too. There are several classes of anti-depressants, and many medications in each class, so it may take you a while to figure out which one works best for you. Prescription medications also take at least a couple of weeks to build up in your system, so do not expect immediate results. Be patient. Many of the side effects can be at their worst in the first couple of weeks, but will fade as your body becomes accustomed to the medication. Also, if you decide to quit taking the anti-depressant, be sure to talk to your doctor first. Many medications require weaning off of them rather than suddenly stop taking them. It also may take some time for the medication to work its way out of your system after you have taken your last pill.

If you opt to go the herbal remedy route instead, there are options for you. St. John's wort and Sam E are very well known herbal anti-depressants. Sam E is much more expensive than St. John's wort, but it can be more effective for some people. If you decide to try one of these herbal remedies, then please only follow the dosage instructions on the bottle, as there is no standard dosage for each pill. Each manufacturer makes different dosages. Also, if you are taking any other medications, be sure to talk to your doctor before starting any medication, herbal or otherwise.

Chapter Seven - Anger

When you were raised by a narcissistic mother, and you finally learn about Narcissistic Personality Disorder, the first reaction usually is relief. Relief that you really are not the terrible person your mother always said you were, and instead it was her projecting her own issues onto you. Then, other emotions kick in, such as grieving. You grieve for your lost childhood, the fact that you were so terribly abused, and the fact that your own mother deliberately hurt you to forward her own selfish agenda.

Eventually, you also get angry over those same things and more.

I learned that anger changes as you heal. For me, for many years I felt very little anger towards those who abused me. Or if I felt any anger, I quickly made excuses as to why what they did was acceptable behavior. Recently though, within the last year or so, I had become very angry at people who have hurt and abused me over the years. Many so-called friends, my narcissistic in-laws, my narcissistic ex husband, an extremely controlling ex boyfriend and even my husband for some dysfunctional behaviors he used to exhibit in our relationship. I also have been angry with my parents, because if they had not raised me the way they had but raised me in a healthy way instead, I would not have grown into a narcissist magnet and willing doormat. And, if I would not have been that way, people would not have thought it was perfectly acceptable to abuse me.

After asking God about it, I believe this to be a normal part of healing from narcissistic abuse. As you heal, naturally your self-esteem improves. And, people with healthy self-esteem have no tolerance for being abused because they know their value. They know they do not deserve to be treated in such a way. Also as you heal, you begin to realize that some behaviors you once thought were normal were in fact abusive. Realizing that will make you angry. Probably about a year ago, I suddenly got very angry with my ex husband's mother because she once intervened in an argument that my ex husband and I had. At the time it happened, I thought this was normal for her to do, since we were living in her home at the time. It took me twenty years to realize just how messed up that situation was. It made me angry she thought she had the right to get involved in our fight, and also that she thought she should tell me how I needed to fix things with her son. She did not say one word to him about him punching her wall, but instead told me I needed to calm him down and apologize to him and her both for making him angry enough to punch her wall.

Also, being the narcissist magnet and doormat type like I was, you are often stuck in more than one abusive relationship at a time. I certainly was. This means you are so busy simply trying to survive with your sanity in tact that you do not have time to deal with your anger properly. You are just trying to get through each encounter with these people with your sanity undamaged. The anger gets shoved into the background, and eventually bubbles to the surface.

So how do you deal with this old anger?

Many people do not believe you should let go of that anger. They say their abuser does not deserve to be forgiven, which admittedly, is true. Some use the Bible, saying that no where in there does it say we need to forgive evil people of their evil deeds, especially when those people do not even acknowledge the hurt they have caused. That amazes me, considering there are so many verses in the Bible that say we need to forgive others. Just a few are: Matthew 6:14-15; Matthew 18:21; Mark 11:25-26; Luke 6:37; Luke 17:3, 4; Luke 23:34; Ephesians 4:32.

I believe the reason that forgiveness is stressed so frequently in the Bible is because it does no one any good if you hold onto the anger. Chances are the person who hurt you does not even know that you are angry. And, narcissists do not care about the feelings of others so even if she knows you are angry, she will not care. She believes that your anger is your problem, even if she is the reason you are angry.

Meanwhile, you are the only one suffering by carrying this anger around. Anger is a very strong emotion that demands to be heard and dealt with. Angry people can become abusive, hurting innocent people who have nothing to do with the reason they are angry in the first place. Or, it can be more self-destructive, such as drinking too much alcohol, doing drugs, eating disorders, depression or physical illnesses like high blood pressure, headaches or digestive problems.

For years, I was angry. I was so tired of being treated as if I did not matter to anyone, and I had to conform to what was expected of me. I felt as if I had no right to confront the people who felt so free to treat me this way, and I was afraid to confront them anyway since I may hurt their feelings. It was incredibly frustrating, and it hurt knowing their feelings were much more important than mine. The anger I felt left me miserable, as I had no way to let it out.

Any time I let any anger or even simple frustration show as a child, my mother scolded me for my terrible temper. "That Bailey temper" is what she called it. My ex husband was not much better. He was allowed to be angry, to punch walls, my car and even our microwave once, but if I was angry, I was wrong. My current husband has drastically improved, but he too had issues with me being angry when we first got together, because he grew up with seeing his father's explosive rages on a constant basis. Anger scared and upset him, so he did not want me to express any anger. As a result, I learned to keep my anger buried deep inside, which left me depressed, even to the point of being suicidal.

Please learn from my mistakes and learn healthy ways to let your anger out! I would not wish the misery of holding in anger on anybody.

Some people are fortunate. They are able to ask God to help them let things go and forgive, and then it is over for them. The anger is gone. Honestly I envy those people, because I am not so fortunate. I have to feel things to fully process them, and only then can I let things go. If you are like me, read on. I will share some tips of what works for me below.

What helps me mostly is prayer. I talk to God about it. I also write it out in my journal if I do not feel like talking about it. Either way, I let it all out to God. He listens (or reads) without judgment, no matter how ugly what I say is.

You also can talk to someone non-judgmental, such as a good friend, a close relative or a counselor.

I also ask God to help me get rid of the anger. I certainly do not want to carry it around, and He wants us to forgive our enemies. Since it is so beneficial for us to forgive, you can rest assured He wants to help you to release that anger.

Do not forget to ask God to comfort you. This process is not a pleasant one - a little comfort can go a long way in helping you to get through it all.

Praying for the narcissist in your life is very helpful, too. I know it is hard, but it helps you to let go of the anger you feel for them. Give it a try!

And, do not judge yourself for this. Anger happens, and it is perfectly understandable. You have valid reasons for being angry! Do not criticize yourself for feeling something perfectly normal and understandable under the very abnormal circumstances of narcissistic abuse!

Chapter Eight - Anger At Those Who Did Not Help

When I was growing up and being abused by my narcissistic mother, it never crossed my mind that anyone could or should help me. It was not until things got really bad when I was seventeen that I started looking for help for ways to deal with the abuse. I thought I was missing something, and someone had to know a way I could fix my mother's abusive behavior. I figured I had to be doing something wrong or missing some obvious solution to this problem, aside from caving in, doing only what she wanted me to do and basically being her puppet. No one helped me. No one even said she was abusive. In fact, no one really even cared about what I was going through, let alone helped me.

At the time, this was not a problem for me. I did not really think anything of it. As I got older though, when I was around thirty, I realized the severity of the damage that was done to me. I also really began to get angry. I was not only angry about being abused, but I was very angry at certain people who did nothing to help me. I became angry at my high school guidance counselor, who condescendingly told me "That doesn't sound so bad" when I explained to her about my mother screaming verbal abuse at me daily. I also became angry at my friends (using that term loosely) that I tried to talk to who shrugged it off, not even offering me any comfort. I became angry with my ex husband as well. It was because I wanted to date him that my mother's abuse escalated. She did not want me dating anyone, but especially him since she hated him upon first sight. He knew this, yet continued not only to push a relationship with him, but to tell me how hard it was for him that I was me being abused. I also got very angry with my father. He defended me to my mother twice in my life that I know of, and twice, she screamed at him for it. To this day he reminds me of how hard that was for him, completely disregarding what she did to me that led up to their situation. There have been many other times that he has told me how he could not do anything to stop her. He says when I was a very small child, she told him that she would be in charge of disciplining me, and he needed to stay out of it. He claimed that meant he could do nothing to help me. When I was going through the worst of my mother's abuse, he often told me how hard it was for him that I was going through this. I was the one being abused, yet I had to comfort him instead of him offering me comfort. In fact, he still does this sometimes to this day; he looks for reassurance from me about my problem when I am the one in crisis.

Does my story sound familiar to you? Do you too feel angry at those who let you down, who failed to offer you any help during your painful experience with narcissistic abuse? If so, you are not alone! I think this is quite common with those who were abused by narcissistic parents.

I think as you begin to heal, you see things differently. You finally realize that is was not your fault that you were abused, and nothing you could have done would have stopped the abuse. These are fantastic revelations, because you finally are able to stop blaming yourself. Also, as you learn about narcissism, you understand that the terrible things said about you were not true. They were said to beat you down, to control you and to make the narcissist feel better about herself. This helps to build your self-esteem, when you realize you are not that horrible human being you were told you were. As your self-esteem gets healthier, for the first time in your life, you realize you have value. Once that happens, at some point it clicks in your mind that no one helped you as an abused child, and it makes you angry.

Children need to be taken care of, so what happened? Why did no one think you were worth helping, worth saving from such a terribly abusive situation? Did people really think it was not so bad or did they think you were making things up? Why did people not believe you or ignore your requests for help? Why did everyone defend or ignore your narcissistic mother's horrible behavior, or make excuses for it, even when they say first hand how bad she could be?

So many questions can go through your mind, and there are rarely good answers to them. It can be absolutely infuriating! It can be very hard too, because if you grew up with a narcissistic parent, you learned early that your anger was a terrible thing. It should be stifled, and never shown. As a result, you have been stifling your anger for years, never expressing it or even feeling it. When it finally does start coming to the surface, it feels extremely foreign. It can feel like now that it has come up, it never can be controlled or it never will go away. It is very scary. Thankfully, it can be controlled, and it will go away once you have learned to deal with it properly.

In the last chapter, I discussed ways to help deal with anger in a healthy way. Those ways also can help you to deal with your anger at those who left you to suffer through narcissistic abuse on your own.

Chapter Nine - Blaming God

Going through narcissistic abuse really affects every area of your life. In many cases, it can even leave you feeling angry at God or doubting His existence or even both. If you grew up in the church or your narcissistic parents claimed to be good Christians, the odds of this happening increase drastically.

When I was growing up, my narcissistic mother told me that good people go to Heaven, and bad people go to Hell. I had no idea what defined good and bad. I wondered what this meant exactly. If you cheat on a diet, did that mean you are Hell-bound? What if you are not paying attention and trip over a bump in the sidewalk? That is a mistake, but did it mean God would send you to Hell? Did cheating on a test count, even if you were desperate to get a decent grade so you did not fail the class? It all seemed preposterous to me, and God must be cruel to make such ridiculous rules like this. I felt like He was just waiting on me to mess up so He could have a good excuse to send me to Hell.

Then as I got older and my mother's abuse increased, I figured God must not exist. How could He exist and allow her to do these horrible things to me? I heard some people say God loves everyone, but I certainly did not feel loved. I was angry at Him for letting me go through what I did every day, but somehow I did not think He could exist either. It sounds very strange, I know, but that is how I felt.

I think confusion about and anger at God are quite common in those who have survived abuse at the hands of a narcissist, so if this describes you, just know that you are not alone!

I am incredibly grateful to say God got my attention in 1995 and showed me how wrong my views were. A few months later in February, 1996, I accepted Jesus as my Savior. Since then, He has taught me so much.

One thing God taught me is that although He does not want people to abuse others, they have the freedom to choose to do so. During those times, He is still with you, enabling you to get through. I know it may not feel like it, but it is still very true. Psalm 23:4 states, **"Yea, though I walk through the valley of the shadow of death, I will fear no evil: for thou art with me; thy rod and thy staff they comfort me." (KJV)**

God also will give you strength not only to endure what you have endured, but to help you to heal, which sometimes, can feel just as hard as living through abuse. Philippians 4:13 says, **"I have strength for all things in Christ Who empowers me [I am ready for anything and equal to anything through Him Who infuses inner strength into me; I am self-sufficient in Christ's sufficiency]." (AMP)**

God also does the most amazing thing. He can make good come from your terrible situation. I know, there are plenty of times it seems like there is no possible way for any good to come from being abused by a narcissist. It really can, though! Romans 8:28 says, **"And we know that all things work together for good to them that love God, to them who are the called according to his purpose." (KJV)** We will focus on this in more detail in the future chapter twenty six entitled "Trauma Changes You" and in chapter thirty two entitled "The Good Things."

Rest assured, Dear Reader, that God truly does care. He understands your pain and all of the devastating hurt that being abused by a narcissist has caused you. He did not abandon you although it probably felt that way at the time. He has been with you from the moment you were conceived, and even before that really, because He planned for you to be the way you are, born when you were. Although He never wanted what happened to you to happen, He will be glad to help you work through it all, and to bless you by making some good come of it.

You are a blessing to God. He loves you so much, and is proud of you.

Chapter Ten - Feeling Robbed

Recently, a very strange thing happened in my life. A lady driving her motorcycle on the road in front of my home laid it down as she swerved to avoid hitting a car. She was injured but not too badly considering the fact she was in a motorcycle accident, I'm happy to say. Her bike also survived with very minimal damage. The strange part of this was not her accident, since many of them happen on the road in front of my home. The strange part was what it did to me.

This accident got me to thinking about how much I used to love motorcycles. Shortly before we got married, I broke up with my ex husband. During that time, he got a motorcycle, he said because he knew I would not like it. I knew someone who died in a motorcycle accident, and they scared me because of that. After we got married, he kept the bike, and I rode with him many times. I began to enjoy motorcycles a great deal. In fact, while we were living with his parents in 1993, I got my permit, and fully intended to get my motorcycle license. My ex even bought a pretty 1982 Honda Nighthawk that I was going to drive. Unfortunately, that did not happen though.

One day when we were out riding, a sudden rainstorm came up. As I was following my ex on his father's bike, my ex's bike slid out from under me on a turn. The rain made the oil on the road very slick, and as a novice rider, I lost control. It was so slick, several cars that passed over that same spot also slid a bit. Thankfully I was not badly injured, just very sore for a while, and the bike's only injury was a bent clutch handle.

My ex told me then that I could not tell his mother about my accident. He said if I did, she would not let me get my license. This baffled me since I was twenty-two years old and she was not my mother. She had no control over me, but he said she did.

Once I was feeling better, I wanted to ride again, in spite of my ex husband's protests. I was afraid if I did not ride, I would become too fearful to get my license, maybe not even wanting to ride with him again. My ex parked his bike in the front yard for me, on the slightly wet grass. I got on it and it promptly fell over. My foot slipped on the wet grass, and his bike was a bit too tall for me anyway, so it was not a big surprise this happened. After this he told me I could not handle a motorcycle and would not let me get my license. His mother agreed after seeing me fall off the bike in her front yard. I had no other means to get my license, and to this day, still do not have a motorcycle driver's license.

I had not thought about this incident in many years, until the recent motorcycle accident in front of my home triggered the memory of this event. Once I thought about it, I began to feel very angry at my ex husband. I felt robbed of something I wanted. I also realized how much he took from me. Before we got married, he was always asking for money from me (he gave his mother his entire paycheck), even knowing how tight my money was. He mostly though tried to rob me of my personhood by acting like I was deeply flawed, and changing me into the person he wanted me to be.

I also realized how robbed I was by my narcissistic parents when I was growing up. They robbed me of a happy, normal childhood by expecting me to be and do what they wanted. They robbed me of inner peace by putting me under tremendous pressure to take care of them emotionally via emotional incest while my feelings were invalidated regularly. They robbed me of family when my mother would not allow me to spend time with my father's family and told me my grandparents were ashamed of me.

As these things went through my mind, I realized feeling robbed must be pretty common among those who have survived narcissistic abuse. I asked some other survivors, and found it is true. Many survivors feel robbed of various things by the narcissist in their lives. Some things that have come to my mind and that they mentioned include feeling robbed of:

- Being allowed simple human rights, such as the right to feel, to dream, to have wants and needs.
- Their identity, because their parent or partner wanted to change them into someone else.
- Their self-esteem, because their narcissist destroyed it.
- Simple things that most parents provide for their children, such as a first car, college education or wedding.
- A home they once loved, but grew to hate due to the bad memories attached to it.
- Mental health. Being subjected to gaslighting and constant scathing criticisms that the end result was C-PTSD.
- Possessions, such as in cases of their narcissist giving away their things without their permission, destroying their possessions in a fit of rage and blaming them for making them destroy the items, or even making them feel

crazy, wrong or stupid for wanting to keep something of theirs.

Does any of this sound familiar to you? Do you feel robbed by the narcissist in your life as well?

Since this revelation is still very new to me, I am still working on how to deal with it. What I am learning so far is that feeling robbed makes a person very angry, and with good reason. Since anger was covered in chapter seven, I see no point in rehashing ways to deal with anger. I will say that I believe it is best to accept the fact that you are angry, acknowledge that you have a right to be angry, and deal with that anger to the best of your ability using the suggestions I made in chapter seven.

I also think that you can get back much of what was stolen from you. Not from the narcissist, but from God. Isaiah 61:3 says, ***"To appoint unto them that mourn in Zion, to give unto them beauty for ashes, the oil of joy for mourning, the garment of praise for the spirit of heaviness; that they might be called trees of righteousness, the planting of the Lord, that he might be glorified." (KJV)*** God can and will bless you and restore to you what was stolen by narcissistic abuse. If you feel robbed of having a decent childhood, as an adult, God can instill a playful spirit in you. He can show you how to play and have fun like you should have done as a child. For a while now, I have been collecting some items from my childhood that I enjoyed. My husband and I play old video games together sometimes at a local arcade that has vintage games from our childhood. I also amuse myself alone by playing various games online. Playing is fun!

You can give yourself certain things as well. If you were robbed of a college education, why not look into going now, as an adult? There are many scholarships and grants available. Did your narcissistic parents refuse to give you a wedding? Then renew your vows with your spouse in a ceremony like you wish you could have had, inviting only those people you are especially close to. Did your narcissistic parents give away a childhood possession of yours that you treasured? Then look for a replacement. Vintage toys are readily available online. Why not find one to replace the one you lost? And, do not forget to play with it once you get it!

    If you trust God, He can return to you much of what was taken from you, and give you a joy that no human can give you. He is doing it for me, and most certainly will do it for you as well. Claim Isaiah 61:3 as being written for you. Trust that God does as He says He will do, and then be prepared to be blessed.

Chapter Eleven - Bitterness And Negativity

Being subjected to narcissistic abuse can turn anyone bitter and negative, especially about one's self. How could it not? You are inundated by a huge amount of negativity. You are constantly being told everything that is wrong with you, that you cannot do anything right and what you want to do is wrong. You eventually see nothing good about yourself, because the constant criticisms have become a part of you. You honestly believe that you are the stupid, fat, ugly, weird, lazy, useless person you were told that you were. It is normal to think that way. Most people believe something if they hear it often enough, especially when the person telling them this information acts as if what she says is fact rather than her opinion. When someone says something with such conviction as a narcissist does, it is normal to take it as fact, especially when that person is your parent.

Narcissistic abuse also can turn a person very negative. You are so hurt constantly, that your attitude about people becomes negative. You do not expect them ever to show kindness or concern. You only expect them to hurt you somehow.

I also have not known one narcissist who was positive in any way. If there is any possible negative scenario, they will find it. They remind me of that little boy in the movie, "Kindergarten Cop." In one scene, the teacher is frustrated. This boy asks him what is wrong. The teacher says he has a headache. The boy responds with, "It might be a tumor." It is a funny scene, but only in a movie. People who are that negative in real life are utterly depressing. If you live with one of these "could be a tumor" people, the bad attitude tends to rub off on you.

I was no exception. I was very bitter and negative for a long time. I was not happy either, although I had a few moments of happiness periodically.

Thankfully, God has changed me. He can change you too.

Developing a close relationship to God was vital for me. As I began to have faith in Him, I began to trust that He would teach me who He says I am, and to enable me to become a good person (since I believed I was a terrible person). This helped me to reject all of the awful things that people said I was and that I once believed, and gain a healthier self-esteem. Admittedly, I still have some trouble in this area once in a while, but it is a thousand times better than it ever was, and is still improving. My healthier self-esteem also helps me to look at criticisms objectively now instead of blindly assuming the critical person is right.

Getting closer to God also has helped me to be more positive. I would not say I am an optimist, but a realist now rather than a pessimist as I once was. I do not automatically expect things to go wrong, but I know that is a possibility. I also know with God in my life, even if things go wrong, He will help me to get through somehow. With God in my life, I now have hope, where I had none without Him.

Learning about Narcissistic Personality disorder helped me to release the negativity and bitterness I felt as well. I am very grateful that God pointed me in this direction, and continually leads me to very helpful information about it. I have learned so much in the last few years about their bad behavior, and the motivations behind it. I learned that their behavior is not about me, it is about them. Like every single thing narcissists do, it is about them.

The awful things that these people told me was them trying to bring me down to make themselves feel better, since hurting others makes narcissists feel powerful. They also most likely were projecting their feelings about themselves onto me. (Projection is a common tool of narcissists. It allows the narcissist to get mad about their flaws without accepting the fact they have the flaws. They blame you instead for being that way, which enables them to get angry about the behavior without accepting that they act that way.)

Leaning on God and letting Him guide you is truly helpful in overcoming a negative attitude and bitterness brought on by narcissistic abuse. In all honesty, I cannot imagine where I would be without His help right now. I would encourage you to ask Him for help in these areas. He truly wants to help you!

Chapter Twelve - Anxiety

Anxiety is a part of life that happens every day in all kinds of situations. Meeting your new boyfriend's family, moving or starting a new job can trigger anxiety, which is totally normal.

Sometimes, however, something goes wrong, and anxiety tries to take over your life. It is very typical for those with narcissistic parents to have issues with anxiety. Engulfing narcissistic mothers in particular create a great deal of anxiety in their children. These mothers treat their child as if the child is completely incapable of doing anything right. She has to do whatever it is because the child obviously cannot to it. This type of behavior leads the child to believe she is completely incompetent, which creates a tremendous amount of anxiety, even in her adult years.

Narcissistic mothers also create an enormous amount of anxiety in their child because the child knows from day one that she is there to take care of her mother and to please her. She must anticipate her mother's needs, and if she knows what her mother wants before her mother knows, all the better. If she does not, she is on the receiving end of a vicious narcissistic rage. While this creates a child who grows into a sensitive adult who is good at reading people, understanding the feelings of others and anticipating the needs of others, it also creates an enormous amount of anxiety. Living under the constant stress of that does not disappear once the child grows up and moves out of her mother's home.

Anxiety comes in many forms. GAD, or General Anxiety Disorder is where a person feels anxious constantly for no specific reason. They cannot relax, and are anxious about everything. Concentration and sleep are very difficult for them. They also may experience frequent trips to the bathroom, muscle tension, aches, tremors and irritability.

Obsessive Compulsive Disorder, also known as OCD, is when unwanted, intrusive thoughts replay constantly, often forcing a person into unhealthy behaviors. Someone with OCD may lock a door, and check it fifteen times to be sure it is locked, or wash their hands so often, their skin becomes raw. Some people exercise compulsively

There is also social anxiety, which is when you experience anxiety when it comes to dealing with people. Even a simple thing like calling to see if a store carries a certain item can be very challenging or impossible. People with social anxiety avoid being the center of attention at all costs. They often experience such physical symptoms as blushing, rapid heart beat, sweating, trembling, muscle tension and aches, confusion and upset stomach. Some cases of social anxiety go to an extreme of agoraphobia, where the person is afraid to leave home.

Phobias are a specific fear, such as a fear of water, snakes, spiders or height, that make a person willing to go to extreme measures to avoid such things.

Many people with anxiety troubles also have panic attacks. Your breath comes in short and rapid waves, your chest muscles get tight and can be painful, blood pressure goes up, and you get dizzy. You may feel as if you are going to pass out. Some people think they are having a heart attack instead of a panic attack when they have their first one. I did. It was terrifying!

Thankfully, there are some ways that can help you cope with anxiety.

- A close relationship with God is vital. During times of anxiety, run to your Heavenly Father for comfort. Tell Him how you feel. He understands, and will help you to calm down.
- Ask God where your anxiety is coming from. It may simply be a dysfunctional way of thinking rather than something physically wrong. And, ask Him to heal you.
- Natural remedies are very helpful. Valerian root, lemon balm, kava kava and chamomile are all natural anti-anxiety remedies. St. John's Wort is an anti-depressant, but it can help with anxiety as well. If you opt for these natural remedies, be sure to follow the instructions on the bottle closely. Different manufacturers make their herbal supplements differently. Lavender is commonly used in aromatherapy for anxiety. You can place a lavender sachet in your pillow case to help you sleep or use lavenders essential or scented oils around your home.
- Many people find prescription anti-anxiety medications helpful. General practitioners can prescribe it, as can psychiatrists. Be sure to learn about the possible side effects before trying any though, as many psychiatric medications have a long list of possible side effects.

- Talk about what is bothering you. Confide in safe, caring, non-judgmental people or write in a journal.
- Massages by either a professional or your spouse will help to reduce anxiety greatly.
- Spend time outside. Nature is very restorative. One of my favorite things to do is look at the stars on a clear, warm night. It brings so much peace, and is so beautiful. Take a walk in the woods or on the beach, thoroughly taking in all of the beauty surrounding you. Work in a garden, marveling at the beauty of God's creations.
- Try to keep a healthy perspective. Can what you are anxious about hurt you? Can it harm your life in any way? Will it make a difference in the grand scheme of things? No? Then why be anxious about it? Try to release your anxiety, and ask God to help you do so if you cannot do it on your own.
- Get creative. It really can relax you to get creative. Paint, write poetry, crochet.
- Get a pet. Animals are wonderful companions. They offer unconditional love and friendship. Just be certain that you have the time, energy and finances to devote to a pet, as they depend on you to take good care of them.
- A service animal is another possibility. Many people with Post Traumatic Stress Disorder have service animals, and have great results with them. They can keep you grounded

during flashbacks, remind you when it is time to take medications, offer comfort and protect you in uncomfortable public situations. If this sounds like a good option for you, talk to your therapist or psychiatrist about the possibility of obtaining a service animal.

Chapter Thirteen - Shock

One odd, yet common, thing I have experienced myself and noticed many times in others who have been through narcissistic abuse is a feeling of shock and astonishment that does not seem to want to go away.

At first, the shock is because of learning about Narcissistic Personality Disorder. Finally, you realize it is not you! You are OK, but your abuser is not. After all these years, that knowledge is shocking because you were absolutely certain you were the problem. Now that you realize that you are not the problem, although it is a relief, it is also a very big shock to your beliefs.

Then as time goes on, and you learn more and more about NPD, you are shocked to see just how pervasive it is. It seems to permeate every single part of a narcissist's being. Every single little thing a narcissist does in her life is only because of the narcissism. A narcissist does nothing for any other reason than to care for her narcissism. It is shocking when you learn that so much can stem from one character problem.

It is also shocking when your eyes are opened, and you realize the great lengths that your narcissistic mother will go to in order to further her agenda. You once took these things in stride, thinking her outrageous behavior was normal or even making excuses for it. Suddenly you realize that they are not normal, are in fact very far from normal. You even realize that her behavior is abnormal, and it is very hard to wrap your mind around. During lunch with my parents once, my father and I inadvertently left my mother out of a short conversation. Apparently this was a problem for my mother, even though my father and I had not done it intentionally. My mother decided to get the attention focused back on her. She began to sing the song "Oklahoma!" loudly until my father and I focused our attention on her strange behavior and abandoned our conversation. My father began talking to her, asking what was wrong with her, and she was very happy, since she was once again the focus of all of the attention at the table. This happened many years ago, and at the time, I did not think anything of this madness. Yes, it was strange, but not really all that strange for my mother since she often showed some strange behavior. Now that I understand narcissism, however, I feel shocked when I think of the way she acted that day, and how utterly bizarre this incident was.

There is also a deep shock that there can be so much evil contained in one person. It is especially shocking that anyone would aim that evil at one's own child. It is only natural that a mother love, protect and care for her child. Look at animals. Cats for example, are wonderful mothers. It is a beautiful thing watching a mother cat with her babies. There is so much love there between the mother and babies, and it is very obvious that the babies know exactly how loved and safe they are in their mother's presence. They care for their babies' needs, they teach them, they play with them, they snuggle them, and they shower them with a great deal of love. This is exactly what a mother, animal or human, is supposed to do. Narcissistic mothers, however, are exactly the opposite - they do not care about their child's needs, they rarely teach them anything, they do not play with or cuddle their child nor do they shower the child with love.

Instead, they see their child as a mere tool to be used as they need, or an extension of themselves, only to be molded into whatever the narcissistic mother wants that child to be. This goes so completely against what is natural, and it is nearly impossible to comprehend, even when you have lived with it. The shock of it never seems to go away completely.

If you are someone who understands narcissism and has worked on healing from narcissistic abuse, yet still find yourself feeling shocked sometimes, you are totally normal. I have not met one person yet who does not feel shock and quite often, no matter how much they have read about narcissism or how many years they have known about it.

Chapter Fourteen - Absolute Thinking

A common phenomenon with children who were abused by narcissists is they grow up thinking in absolutes. Everything is either black or white, with no gray areas. For example, if you forget your husband's birthday, you may tell yourself that you are a bad wife. People who do not think in this absolute way would feel bad, obviously, but they would also realize that they also had a thousand other things going on which made the date simply slip their mind.

This unbending kind of thinking is not healthy for one's self-esteem. When you show yourself no mercy for mistakes, only berating yourself for them, it takes a definite toll on your self-esteem.

You also allow no room for changes when your thinking is so rigid. You feel you should look or act a certain way, or like or dislike certain things, and when changes happen, you harshly criticize yourself for these changes.

You do not forgive yourself if you gained a few pounds or do something embarrassing like slip on the ice in front of people, but instead tell yourself you are fat and clumsy. This causes a great deal of harm to your self-esteem.

Absolute thinking also can damage relationships or even mean you miss out on good relationships. As an example, my mother hates smoking and people who smoke. She has put her beliefs on me on this topic ever since I can remember. She was especially hard on my paternal grandparents who smoked for many years. It did not seem logical to me that smokers were bad, dirty, disgusting people since my grandparents were not that way at all. I am glad I do not think the way my mother does. I have had some very good friends who just happen to smoke. Unlike her, I do not believe smoking makes someone a bad person. I believe a person's behavior can make them bad instead. If I believed as my mother does, I would be missing out on having some very special, wonderful people in my life.

I would like to encourage you to think about your beliefs. Do you think in black and white terms? If so, stop! It is not good for you!

To start with, ask God for help. Help to be more open minded, to question before judging. He will do so and do so gladly. Psalm 19:14 says, **"Let the words of my mouth, and the meditation of my heart, be acceptable in thy sight, O Lord, my strength, and my redeemer." (KJV)** This can be a wonderful prayer to pray.

You also need to start challenging your thoughts. If you beat yourself up for making mistakes, it is time to remember that everyone makes mistakes. You are no different than other people. If no one made mistakes, there would be no need for Jesus. Making mistakes does not make you a bad person or a failure - it makes you human.

If you are extremely fast to criticize yourself, then I urge you to stop. When you tell yourself that you are too fat, stupid, a screw up, or whatever terrible things you say to yourself, stop for a moment and tell yourself why those views are dead wrong. It may be hard at first to know why those views are wrong, so ask God to help you. Ask Him to tell you why those views are incorrect, and then listen for the answer. He will speak to you if you only listen.

If you find yourself thinking someone or something is bad, then stop for a moment and ask yourself why you feel this way. Does this belief stem from something you learned from your narcissistic mother? If so, then why does she feel this way? Does this make sense to you? Can you honestly say you agree with her logic? If not, then discard her feelings and form your own opinion! You are entitled to your own opinion just as much as anyone else is!

This type of absolute thinking has been a big hindrance in my emotional healing. I cannot count how many times I told myself that I should be over this by now, I am just feeling sorry for myself, and other dysfunctional and downright abusive things. I even have scolded myself many times for having C-PTSD since other people have had it much worse than I, it was "only" narcissistic abuse and other ridiculous things. I realized that this is abusive to myself, that I was abusing myself just like the narcissists in my life have done. I was continuing the dysfunctional cycle, and it had to stop!

Have you done the same thing to yourself while you are healing?

Always remember that healing is a very individual experience. No two people will heal in the same way at the same speed, even if they experience exactly the same trauma. There is nothing black and white about healing. It is a very gray area.

Chapter Fifteen - Stifled Creativity

Narcissists cannot stand anyone who is creative, who thinks outside the box if you will, and will do their absolute best to destroy that person's beliefs in their creative talents. The goal is to make the creative person feel as if she is wrong, bad or crazy for her gifting.

Narcissists are insanely envious of the fact that creative people have unique and original ideas, ideas that may gain them positive attention, which is why they will so harshly criticize those ideas and the people who have them.

Then there is the fact that many people admire those with a great deal of creativity. They might get either good or bad attention that the narcissist believes should be for her. So, in the narcissist's eyes, this means the creative person is deliberately stealing her attention. How dare that creative person steal her attention! She must pay!

Since very creative people tend to think differently than your average person, there is also the very real possibility that a creative person will catch on to the fact that how the narcissist treats the creative person is not normal. What if that happens? Will you call the narcissist out on her abusive and bad behavior? Or, you may expose the narcissist's true persona. People may not think as highly of her if you do that, so that must not happen at all costs!

If you are an exceptionally creative person, you usually do not fit in with most people. Your unique talents, ideas and how you think make you a little different, which can make you feel awkward or possibly even damage your self-esteem if you are criticized for it enough. Narcissists can sniff out insecurity as easily as a bloodhound on a scent trail. Insecure people make the easiest targets for narcissists. A confident person is much more difficult to beat down, if not impossible, which is why they aim for people with at least a little insecurity.

Not one bit if this is your fault, but the narcissist will act like every single little bit of it is.

I think because of growing up with such a critical, narcissistic mother, I have issues with expressing my creativity to this day. I can see something that inspires me. I want to make something like it, draw a picture of it or write an article or book about it, but when I go to do it, sometimes I just shut down. The creative idea I had only five minutes ago vanishes completely. Even looking at whatever it was that inspired me does not bring it back. For example, one day recently, I decided I was going to sketch a tea pot. Maybe even a tea service. In my mind, I had a picture of what I wanted the tea pot to look like, but when I got out my pencils and paper, the idea was completely gone. I could not even think of what shape to make the tea pot, let alone any more details. It was extremely frustrating!

The good news is the more I heal from the narcissistic abuse, the less frequently this shutting down thing happens. I am sure that is how it will happen for you as well. Also, when it does happen now, it is not as severe as it once was. Now I can jot down a note about something I want to write about and later when I look at it, I often remember exactly what the note was about, even if I wrote very few details with it. It used to be that I had to write a lot of details and hope that later on when I went to write, I would be able to write what I wanted to. I am very grateful for the improvements!

I have learned too, to remind myself that I have every right to express my creativity in whatever ways I desire, just like any other person. Everyone needs a creative outlet. Creativity is healthy, it gives you more peace and joy, it helps you to relax, and it helps you to feel accomplished. Just because someone in your life has not approved of what you do creatively, that does not mean you are wrong, stupid or bad for doing what you enjoy doing.

This brings me to another point. When you being to express yourself creatively, chances are you will be exceptionally critical of your efforts. That is very typical considering you have been exposed to narcissistic abuse. Narcissists criticize their victims so much and in so many ways, their victims often become extraordinarily critical of themselves. They become perfectionists. While they usually have reasonable expectations of everyone else they know, they cannot stand if they make a mistake, no matter how small, and will berate themselves for that mistake. When you are doing something, try not to be so critical. Look at your project objectively, as if it was a friend's project instead of yours. Also remember, you are just beginning this endeavor. No one starts out at an expert level! It takes time.

I used to love to draw when I was growing up. I got away from it by my mid teens though. Recently, I decided to get back into it. Honestly, I am not as talented as many of the other very artistic members of my family. I have an aunt and cousin who are wonderfully artistic. Their sketches are amazing. However, as I practice, I am improving. I mentioned this to my aunt recently who encouraged me to keep trying, because that is how I will find my voice.

If you want to start expressing the natural creativity inside you, then I would like to encourage you to do just that. It may be awkward at first. Keep going, and you too will find your voice! And, if you do not with this particular endeavor, so what? There are other creative things you can do. You do not have to paint if you find you are not happy with the results. Instead, you can do needlepoint, woodworking, yarn crafts, calligraphy, clay modeling or a host of other things. If you are running low on ideas or motivation, wander through a craft store. They always carry products for a huge variety of crafts. Gentlemen, craft stores are not just for the ladies! Many carry things that men may enjoy as well, such as model cars and airplanes, slot cars, wood projects, and more. Craft stores do not just carry artificial flowers! There is plenty in there to keep you men amused as well as us ladies.

And another thing, Gentlemen, crafts are not just for the ladies. I remember hearing a long time about a football player who loved to do needlepoint. I know a man who enjoys cross stitch, and is very good at it. Do not disregard the idea of "girly" crafts. You may find you enjoy them a great deal.

Chapter Sixteen - That Vicious Inner Critic

You are too old. You are too fat. That outfit looks horrible on you. You are a terrible mother. You cannot do anything right. You never will amount to anything. You are such a disappointment. Why can't you be more like your sister/cousin/neighbor/classmate? What is wrong with you?

I bet you thought it was just you that heard these awful things, said in your narcissistic mother's voice, in your head on a regular basis. It may surprise you, but it is not just you. Those of us who have been through narcissistic abuse have heard many of those same statements and more.

As I have said many times, narcissistic abuse permeates every fiber of your being. As a result of the constant criticism and gaslighting, you end up with something like a cassette tape player in your mind, playing the same sorry old tapes over and over, reminding you of every flaw you have and every mistake you have made.

Unfortunately, unlike a real cassette tape, these tapes do not wear out after repeated use. You have to destroy them.

You have to think about what you are thinking about. What makes those thoughts start? Once you know what makes them start, you can be prepared for how to deal with them.

How do you respond when they start? Do you take them to heart, feeling badly about yourself? Then it is time to challenge those dysfunctional thoughts. As an example, pretend you made a mistake when cooking dinner. You forgot to add a spice to your main course and it turned out bland because of that. When you hear that tape of your mother telling you that you cannot do anything right, you are stupid, etc., stop accepting that. Tell yourself that is not true. Everyone makes mistakes, and mistakes do not make a person bad, stupid or whatever else she would say to you when you made a mistake. You are no exception. Yes, you goofed, but so what? How is the world going to be made a worse place just because you forgot to put a simple spice in your dinner? Say things to yourself like this, and if it helps, say them out loud. Ask God to tell you the truth in this situation. Ask Him if you are stupid for making the mistake you made, and listen for the answer.

These simple steps do help to quiet the abusive voice in your head. In all honesty, I am unsure if that voice ever stops entirely though. I have been trying to quiet it for many years, and still it pops up from time to time. At least it rears its ugly head much less often than it once did, and that is progress!

Chapter Seventeen - People Pleasing

    Whether you are raised by a narcissist or have been romantically involved with one, you learn early on that their love is earned. Narcissists are oblivious to the concept of unconditional love. Their love (well, what they think of as love anyway) is based on your performance and obedience to them, rather than simply loving you for the wonderful person that you are. Their love has not only strings attached, but also chains, ropes, bungee cords, duct tape…

    Narcissists also love to say and do things to instill the belief in you that it is your job to do for other people, no matter the personal cost to you. As an example, when I was about to marry my husband, I mentioned to my father that once we got married, I wanted to keep my maiden name, Bailey, rather than take my husband's last name, Rug. My father had fits about that. He was so angry with me for wanting to keep my name. I had to take my husband's last name! Hyphenating it was not good enough for him, and neither was replacing my middle name with my maiden name. He said it all was wrong and would upset my husband to keep my maiden name in any form. I argued with him that it was my name, I liked it, I wanted to keep it, and I did not want to share a name with his family since they obviously hated me so much. My husband was not happy with my arguments either since he wanted me to have his last name, but it was my father who pushed this issue the hardest. My father pushed the issue so much in fact, that I took my husband's name upon marrying him to please my father, rather than doing as I wanted. (Bailey-Rug is my pen name, not my legal name.) This made my father happy, but even after seventeen years of living with my husband's last name, I still regret letting him push me into taking it.

It is amazing how deep the people pleasing ways can go once you have been exposed to narcissistic abuse. Just look at the story I told in the last paragraph. I sacrificed something I wanted very, very much for my father's happiness. Something that does not even affect him in the slightest. Doing for other people needs to be done in balance. Yes, you should think of other people, and bless them often. Sometimes, you even should make sacrifices for other people. However, it should not be done at the expense of your inner peace or joy. If giving to others is hurting you physically, emotionally, financially or even spiritually, it is a sign that it has to stop, because not only are you being hurt, the people you are doing so much for are really not being helped. Doing too much for people makes them look to you to get their needs met, instead of taking care of themselves or looking to God for help. That is unfair to you, and it also does not teach the other person to do for himself or herself.

How do you achieve balance in this area? I have found God to be an immeasurable help. I have asked Him to help me to know what I should do and for whom. As a result, He has enabled me to know immediately in my heart if I should or should not do as someone asks of me. He also has helped me to have the strength and courage say no, which is something I never expected I would be able to do.

I also had to realize that I am allowed to say no to things that go against my beliefs or that may hurt in some way. Everyone has the right to have healthy boundaries. No one has the right to expect you to do something that will cause you any type of harm or make you compromise your beliefs, and you have every right to protect yourself from that.

Having balance has helped me also to be able to be a blessing to others with joy rather than a sense of obligation that makes me feel resentful. I used to resent doing for other people, because I felt I had to do it, no matter what, even if it hurt me or went against my beliefs. Now? I do not feel that way. I am able to do for others and enjoy it, or say no without feeling guilty.

It also has enabled me to feel that I am doing whatever I am doing for them more for God than the person, which gives me even more joy than doing for people. Pleasing God is so much more rewarding than pleasing your fellow man!

There are some wonderful Scriptures in the Bible that speak about people pleasing versus God pleasing…

Proverbs 16:7 "When a man's ways please the LORD, he maketh even his enemies to be at peace with him." (KJV)

Galatians 1:10 "For do I now persuade men, or God? or do I seek to please men? for if I yet pleased men, I should not be the servant of Christ." (KJV)

Colossians 3:23 "And whatsoever ye do, do [it] heartily, as to the Lord, and not unto men;" (KJV)

1 Thessalonians 2:4 "But as we were allowed of God to be put in trust with the gospel, even so we speak; not as pleasing men, but God, which trieth our hearts." (KJV)

Chapter Eighteen - Always Apologizing

 When you are subject to narcissistic abuse, you learn early on to apologize freely and often. Whatever the problem, according to your narcissistic mother, you are to blame for it, and you need to apologize.
 When I was nineteen, I had my first nervous breakdown after yet another vicious argument with my mother. When my father got involved and they began to argue in front of me, I could not take it anymore. My mother blamed me for their argument, and it pushed me over the mental edge. I quickly ran from the room and locked myself in the bathroom where I remained catatonic for several hours. When I finally came out, my mother was waiting on me. She grabbed me, hugging me tight, and said, "I forgive you!" Immediately I felt guilty for fighting with her, for walking away from the fight, for avoiding her while I had my breakdown (although I did not know that was what happened to me at the time or the severity of it), and for locking myself in the bathroom. I felt so guilty, that I think I even apologized to her at that point. (My memory is a bit fuzzy of that night, so I am not absolutely positive of this.) I also never told her what happened in the bathroom that night out of fear of upsetting her or having her commit me as she had threatened to do many times before.

Is it not amazing how narcissists can make anything into your fault? My nervous breakdown was not my fault, but yet I felt guilty for having it. I also felt bad for making my mother so angry that night that she pushed me so hard that I had the nervous breakdown. That is really ridiculous since she was in the mood to fight with me the moment I walked into her house that night. I did nothing to make her mad, she was already mad at me before I got home.

I have no doubt that as a victim of narcissistic abuse, you can relate. You were made to feel guilty for things that were not your fault. As a result, you learned to apologize to everyone about everything.

No one should be the one to apologize every time. One person simply cannot be wrong every single time. One person also cannot shoulder the blame for another person's actions, which is what happens regularly to those who constantly apologize. Each person should accept responsibility for their own actions, period.

To stop apologizing for everything, you will need to stop and think. When a situation arises where you are expected to apologize, think for a moment. Ask yourself if you really should apologize. Was it your fault? What did you do wrong? Or is someone blaming you for their actions? If you are unsure, ask God to help you to discern the truth when these situations arise.

If you are feeling pressured to apologize even when you are not at fault, then ignore the pressure. I have noticed most narcissists have a very short attention span. They will get bored quickly with hinting for something if they see it is not working.

If the person does not stop demanding an unfair apology, then calmly use logic. Ask questions, such as, "How is it my fault that you did *fill in the blank*? I don't understand. Please explain to me exactly what I did wrong." Do not let the other person off the hook. Keep calmly asking them to explain themselves. Chances are good that they will get tired of trying to get you to apologize and change the subject.

Chapter Nineteen - An Overdeveloped Sense Of Responsibility

Many adult children of narcissistic parents are extremely responsible people.

Narcissistic parents are the most demanding people you could meet, especially when it comes to their children. They expect their child to please them in every way and meet all of their needs no matter what. They expect the child to take care of their emotional needs (emotional incest) and sometimes physical needs as well. The child is expected to anticipate her narcissistic mother's every whim, preferably even before the mother has it, and cater perfectly to those whims.

If the child of the narcissistic mother fails to do these things perfectly, she is at risk of being on the receiving end of the narcissistic rage, which is a place no one wants to be.

This dysfunctional scenario creates a very overdeveloped sense of responsibility in the child that she carries into adulthood. She feels overly responsible for everyone, not only her narcissistic mother.

I lived this life for many years. Whenever my husband was upset, I felt it was my job to make him feel better. If he had a bad day at work or was angry with his parents, I knew it was my place to make it all better for him. If he snapped at me, it was fine with me, because he needed to get his anger out somehow. Yes, it hurt my feelings but that was not important to me if it helped him. In fact, it would make me try harder to fix him. I did the same dysfunctional thing with other people. I even did this with my mother in-law. I realized one day while visiting her home with my husband that when my father in-law was nasty with her, she got nastier with me. I thought maybe it helped her to get the anger out. I honestly thought I was helping her, letting her treat me like trash. So dysfunctional of me!

I thank God for helping me to change, because I was absolutely terrible in this area and miserable because of it. This was an awful way to live. So much pressure! I am so grateful that God got me away from this dysfunction.

He helped me by teaching me about boundaries. A friend sent me Drs. Henry Cloud and John Townsend's book "Boundaries," and it literally changed my life. Boundaries show you where you end and others begin, which helps you to know what you are and are not responsible for. Once you know that information, you realize it is truly NOT your responsibility to do certain things. It takes a great deal of the burden off of you.

Leaning on God is a tremendous help. I also have asked Him to show me who to help and what to do for the people He wants me to help. He truly will guide you and enable you not to feel guilty if He does not want you to help someone for whatever reason. God does not want you to suffer with feeling you have to fix everyone.

Chapter Twenty - Rejecting Your Femininity

If you are a gentleman reading this book, please do not skip this chapter. I honestly am unsure if this type of thing happens to men as well, but I tend to think it has happened to at least a few men. So while this chapter is written directed at the ladies, it may benefit you as well.

Women who were raised by at least one narcissistic parent often reject their own femininity. Narcissists, whether a parent or romantic partner, are out to destroy you in every way possible, and that includes your femininity. Some narcissists take a great deal of pride in their gender, often flaunting their sexuality, which can turn their victims off. Some children of narcissistic parents see this, and are disgusted by their narcissistic mother's behavior. They decide never to act that way, and therefore reject their own femininity out of fear of turning out like their mother. This happened with my mother. When I was a child, my mother said her mother was very promiscuous when she was growing up, and as a result, my mother turned out very prudish.

Women who survived narcissistic abuse and who reject their own feminine nature often want to be strong to avoid being abused ever again. In their minds, to look and act "girly" to them meant they were not strong. Being girly, as far as they are concerned, meant that they were vulnerable, which is something they simply could not tolerate. This is especially common with victims of sexual abuse.

These women often avoid softness in every possible way. Their clothing color and style are bland colors or sometimes bold, and often in unflattering styles. Even if they dress sexy, it is more a blatantly sexy, provocative style instead of subtly sexy. Their hair may be in a more dramatic style or color instead of soft and feminine.

Others may be like me, and strive to look a certain way to avoid criticism or attention. It bothered me to look not so girly, because I have always enjoyed feminine things, like girly clothing, make up and especially nail polish. I looked the way my mother wanted me to rather than how I wanted to, because my mother harshly criticized me if I was too feminine in any way. I thought it was easier to be less feminine than to be mocked.

I think in addition to my mother observing her mother's promiscuity, my mother also may have been sexually abused at some point in her life, because of her views on sex and femininity. She dresses in a way I think of as mostly gender neutral – neither too feminine nor too masculine, colors are pastel to medium yet none are soft, not much make up, and no clothing that accentuates the positives in her appearance. She also seems disgusted by women who are comfortable in their femininity. She is very critical of them as well as women who dress not feminine enough for her liking. The way my mother dresses pretty much can blend into the background, which is also how I always dressed in my younger days growing up around her.

Growing up, my mother also made sure I knew exactly what being feminine meant to her, and shared her views, not only regarding how I looked. Changing your own oil, fixing a clogged sink or planting a garden are jobs for men, according to her. No woman should stoop to such things. It took me a long time before I could accept the fact that I was feminine whether I was getting a manicure or replacing the thermostat on my car. I finally came to believe that femininity is more a state of mind than the actions you are doing.

Did you know that rejecting your femininity can cause problems? Sexual dysfunction, the inability to enjoy sex or insecurity in relationships can happen. Even menstrual problems can happen. Some women have heavy periods with no known physical cause, and others cannot conceive or carry a baby to full term, also without a known physical cause.

I realize not every woman is the "girly girl" type, and I am not trying to change the non-girly types into being super girly. However, I do want you to consider this possibility, that maybe you rejected your femininity due to how you were treated by your narcissistic mother. Have you rejected your femininity? If so, how have you done it? What made you do such a drastic thing? Do you view being feminine as being weak or vulnerable?

If you have rejected your femininity then it is time for you to reclaim it! Being feminine is not a bad thing at all. In fact, I think of it as a gift. It does not make you weak or stupid. It is something about yourself that you should enjoy. God made you the way you are for a reason. Why not enjoy every part of it that you can enjoy?

To start with, I think you need to figure out what being a woman means to you. If you are unsure, Proverbs 31:10-31 is a great place to start to figure this out. God describes a good woman in the following verses.:

"10 Who can find a virtuous woman? for her price is far above rubies. 11 The heart of her husband doth safely trust in her, so that he shall have no need of spoil. 12 She will do him good and not evil all the days of her life. 13 She seeketh wool, and flax, and worketh willingly with her hands. 14 She is like the merchants' ships; she bringeth her food from afar. 15 She riseth also while it is yet night, and giveth meat to her household, and a portion to her maidens. 16 She considereth a field, and buyeth it: with the

fruit of her hands she planteth a vineyard. 17 She girdeth her loins with strength, and strengtheneth her arms. 18 She perceiveth that her merchandise is good: her candle goeth not out by night. 19 She layeth her hands to the spindle, and her hands hold the distaff. 20 She stretcheth out her hand to the poor; yea, she reacheth forth her hands to the needy. 21 She is not afraid of the snow for her household: for all her household are clothed with scarlet. 22 She maketh herself coverings of tapestry; her clothing is silk and purple. 23 Her husband is known in the gates, when he sitteth among the elders of the land. 24 She maketh fine linen, and selleth it; and delivereth girdles unto the merchant. 25 Strength and honour are her clothing; and she shall rejoice in time to come. 26 She openeth her mouth with wisdom; and in her tongue is the law of kindness. 27 She looketh well to the ways of her household, and eateth not the bread of idleness. 28 Her children arise up, and call her blessed; her husband also, and he praiseth her. 29 Many daughters have done virtuously, but thou excellest them all. 30 Favour is deceitful, and beauty is vain: but a woman that feareth the Lord, she shall be praised. 31 Give her of the fruit of her hands; and let her own works praise her in the gates." (KJV)

I urge you to pray. Ask God to help you stop rejecting your femininity and to gain a healthy understanding of what it means to be female.

For myself, I do not believe being feminine is all about wearing lace and never getting dirty. I believe it is more of a state of mind and how a woman carries herself. A feminine woman can wear classic, modest clothing, wear nude nail polish and have a conservative hair style or she can be covered in colorful tattoos, wear black leather and have green hair.

A feminine woman is strong. She is the rock in her family, the one her husband and child go to for comfort after a rough day, but also she is wise enough to know when she needs to pull back a little to renew her strength or to help them to be more self-reliant.

She is also confident. It radiates gently from her. Fewer things are more attractive than a woman who is comfortable in her own skin. She is attractive not only to men but also to other women because they know she is not going to try to compete with them in any way like some more insecure women will do.

A feminine woman must enjoy being a woman. She embraces the softness about herself with joy.

She appreciates beauty in any form, whether it is a painting hanging in a museum, the first flowers of spring or even a classic car's sleek lines. And, she can spot beauty anywhere. Some people see a run down, abandoned shack, but when the feminine woman looks at it, she sees the building as it once was when it was still a fine, proud home to a happy family.

She takes pride in her appearance, keeping her skin, hair and nails well maintained and in good health. She has a regular beauty ritual. She wears clothing and make up that are well suited for her.

She is soft, strong, gentle, caring, helpful, nurturing, generous, graceful and does everything with integrity and excellence. She is never loud, obnoxious, forceful or rude. She does not skimp on anything she does. She would rather not do something than to do it halfway.

Chapter Twenty One - Physical Affection Can Be Difficult

Even when you love someone deeply, after narcissistic abuse, showing physical affection often can be a challenge.

Those of us who grew up with narcissistic parents either had no physical affection, our parents acting as if we were too disgusting or repulsive to be touched, or we had inappropriate physical affection such as in cases of emotional incest where the parent treats the child more like a romantic partner than a child. Actual sexual contact may or may not be a part of emotional incest, but inappropriate touching definitely is.

If you have been involved with a narcissist romantically, that can skew how you handle physical affection too. Narcissistic partners use sex to get whatever they want, proving themselves prolific lovers which naturally makes you want to please them inside and outside of the bedroom. They often use guilt to make you go along with what they want sexually, even when they know it is not something you want. They also are not above punishing you by withholding sex if they believe that will get them whatever it is that they want. In addition, they also withhold physical affection, such as hand holding or hugs, unless it is something they want.

If you have had the unfortunate experience of both being raised by and later married to a narcissist, no doubt you have trouble with physical affection.

I love my friends. They are awesome. Some are kind of demonstrative with their feelings, and hug me when we get together. It has taken me a long time to get to the point I can mostly tolerate it, but even so, there are times I am very uncomfortable with it. One friend, at her father's funeral, she hugged me and did not want to let go. Very awkward for me, but considering the extremely painful circumstances, I hung in there in spite of my own distressing feelings. I love this lady dearly, and if a simple hug was what would help her during that awful time, I decided would ignore my uncomfortable feelings for her.

Time and healing help to make the uncomfortable feelings of physical affection less awkward. Just be patient with yourself, as this is a normal ramification of narcissistic abuse.

Also, remind yourself that there is nothing wrong with physical affection. You were given a very skewed view of it, but that does not mean it is a bad thing.

And of course, as always, ask God to help you in this area.

Chapter Twenty Two - Being An Introvert

An introvert is someone who is energized by spending time alone rather than spending time around other people. They may love people, but even spending time with the ones they love the most can drain them, if they spend too much time together. They avoid parties and large groups of people whenever possible. Introverts have very few friends, often only a couple of friends that they feel especially close to. They prefer deep, close relationships, and will shun acquaintances or superficial friends. Introverts often keep their thoughts and feelings to themselves, only sharing them with the rare people that they allow close to them. They avoid conflict as much as possible, finding it incredibly awkward and uncomfortable. They like quiet, serene environments. Introverts are very creative individuals, often preferring to express themselves in writing or in another artistic way rather than talking. They think about deeper things in life, and are turned off by the lighter, superficial things. Small talk annoys introverts. Introverts make great friends, because they are sensitive, good listeners, honest, observant, trustworthy and intuitive. They often prefer interacting with people via text messages or email over talking on the phone or meeting in person.

I prefer introverts to extroverts, personally. Being one myself, I am most comfortable with people who understand my need to be alone so often. In fact, my friend since 1988 is also an introvert. Many times when we get together, one of us will ask if the other is ready for some introvert time. This translates to, "I want to go home and be alone." We both understand this all too well, so neither of us is offended by the other's sudden desire to go home, even if it is early into our visit. We always have fun together, but even so, more than a couple of hours and we are both ready for our introvert time. It has nothing to do with our feelings about each other – we just need some quiet time to ourselves.

Extroverts drastically outnumber us introverts, which may be partly why introverts are often misunderstood. There simply are not as many of us compared to extroverts. We also do not discuss ourselves easily or readily with most people, which may contribute to the mystery surrounding introverts. As a result of being misunderstood, introverts are often mislabeled as snobs, pretentious, rude, anti-social and other not so nice things when the truth is, we are just quiet and want to keep to ourselves.

Introversion seems to be very common among children of narcissistic parents. I wonder if it is because they see introverts as easy targets since we can appear meek and quiet. Plus, if we are beaten down, we often withdraw into ourselves, not telling anyone what is wrong. This means the abuse will be kept secret, possibly forever, which is a huge bonus for the narcissist. Or, maybe another possibility is that some of us are not necessarily born introverted, but being abused by a narcissistic parent makes us that way. We have to be meek and quiet to avoid the rages. We also have to be isolated and not talk much to anyone so as not to divulge the secret that we are being abused. Maybe some introverts are made this way instead of being born this way. I am honestly not sure if that is possible or not, but it makes sense to me that it could be possible.

Extroverted people sometimes do not understand introverted ones, and may try to change you. I have experienced that often. Friends have tried to get me to go out more often than I want to, and fail to understand I can be very content not leaving home for a long time. I do not get "cabin fever." Some have criticized me for being this way, saying I need to get out more often, or I need to fix this "problem" I have of being an introvert. Some people also have tried to make me feel guilty as well for not wanting to go spend time with them often. They also assume being quiet and preferring to be alone means depression, which is not the case. Granted, I have battled depression my entire life, but even in good, depression-free times, I still preferred to be alone, and at home. I was still quiet.

As much as your introverted nature wishes to avoid conflict and confrontation, depending on the person who is trying to "fix" your introverted ways, you may have to confront them. I find some extroverts do not understand introverts until you explain things in terms they can relate to. Try telling them that the way they feel around a group of people, is how you feel when you are alone. The thrill they have when they know they are going somewhere where they do not know anyone is that same thrill you feel at the thought of spending an evening at home, alone, with your favorite movie or book. You feel the same way they do, but you simply get to those feelings a different way.

My mother, much like most narcissists, is an extrovert. If she has to stay home for more than a couple of days, she is chomping at the bit to go somewhere, anywhere. She spends a lot of time talking on the phone. She talks to cashiers or sales people in stores. She enjoys window shopping. She is my polar opposite, and we have both changed as we have gotten older. She has become much more extroverted, and I have become much more introverted. The scathing criticisms of others and my mother's lack of understanding of my introverted nature has many times left me feeling like there is something wrong with me. It was not until the last few years I realized that being an introvert is not a bad thing. In fact, I have come to embrace it. I enjoy my alone time to the fullest even if others criticize me for it. I love email and Facebook, because they give me a way to be social without having to leave my home or deal with people in person. I also have begun to enjoy writing even more, because I am able to work all alone, without a boss breathing down my neck, telling me to hurry up or telling me what I am doing wrong.

If you too are an introvert, then please know that nothing is wrong with you! Introversion is simply a personality trait. It does not mean there is something flawed or broken about you. Being an introvert is like being born with blue or hazel or brown eyes. It just happens, and you cannot change it. So why not embrace the quality about yourself and learn to enjoy it?

Chapter Twenty Three - Dissociation

I always thought something was very wrong with me. Sometimes, I would "space out" as I thought of it. I could stare into space and feel a million miles away from everyone and everything. This weird phenomenon would happen at any time, in any place. It is especially scary when it happens when I am driving.

I also have relatively few memories of my childhood. I have come to realize I blocked out a great many things that happened to me. And, the bad things I do remember, I feel an odd disconnect to. Almost as if those things happened to someone other than me, even though I know beyond a shadow of a doubt they happened to me.

For a time after separating from my ex husband, I also developed a short term amnesia several times. I forgot some parts of my life, or I forgot my name and most of my life. The episode would last a day or two. I had to be reminded by my current husband of such things. It happened several times. It was very scary and completely bizarre! I did not realize it at the time, but this amnesia was connected to my "space out" episodes, as were the memories that I had blocked out.

I have learned that my behavior is not something unusual. Instead, it is very common for those who have experienced trauma. The phenomenon is called dissociation.

Dissociation is a coping mechanism designed to help a person to tolerate stress or trauma. Since very few things can be more stressful or traumatic than living through narcissistic abuse, I would bet that many narcissistic abuse survivors also dissociate.

It is especially common with victims of sexual assault to dissociate. Those who have been through repeated assaults, such as in cases of living with a husband or father who repeats his abuse regularly, often describe learning how to do something that they describe as leaving their bodies while their abuser assaults them. This enables them to endure the terrible things as he does them. They somehow have learned how to control dissociating, and use it to help them in times of trauma.

Dissociation is a very common symptom of Post Traumatic Stress Disorder and Complex Post Traumatic Stress Disorder.

Since it is a continuum, dissociation can include a mild detachment from your surroundings, to episodes of amnesia (like I described that happened to me) or even developing an alternative personality, what was once known as Multiple Personality Disorder (now known as Dissociative Identity Disorder).

Dissociation is not a sign of weakness, as was originally thought by the French philosopher and psychologist, Pierre Janet. He treated many patients who experienced trauma and they dissociated, but he never made the connection between trauma and dissociation for some reason.

Many people who were chronically abused as children and in particular those abused starting at a very young age dissociate, and have for most of their lives. It is very common, but not all victims of chronic child abuse dissociate.

From my personal experience, I have learned that the more I heal, the less I dissociate. I also have not experienced any more amnesiac episodes since 1996, and I no longer repress painful memories. I have learned healthier coping skills, and no longer assume the blame for "making" another person hurt or abuse me. Now I realize the abusive person is the one with the problem. Normal people do not deliberately hurt other people. This knowledge along with increased self-esteem that tells me I do not deserve to be treated this way have all been incredibly helpful for helping the dissociation to slow down drastically.

I have noticed something though. I am unsure if this will help anyone reading this book, but just in case it will, I am going to include it.

I realized that since I became sick with carbon monoxide poisoning last February, I am dissociating more now than I once did prior to getting sick, although I do not think quite as much as I did as a child and young adult. Some of the psychological symptoms of carbon monoxide poisoning include irritability, moodiness, behaving in an especially sensitive, overly emotional way and it often changes your personality. In many cases, brain damage also occurs due to the lack of oxygen that is delivered in your body caused by carbon monoxide poisoning. If you already have mental health problems, you are much more likely to experience the psychological symptoms than someone without any mental illness. Since I already had Complex Post Traumatic Stress Disorder prior to getting carbon monoxide poisoning, that is most likely why I have experienced all of those psychological changes. Some of the changes have actually been surprisingly good, and I appreciate them. For example, I am beginning to express my emotions more than I ever have before. But, I also started to dissociate on almost a daily basis right after getting sick, whereas it was much less frequent prior to getting sick. It only seems logical that the carbon monoxide poisoning is what made the dissociation worse.

If you too have experienced carbon monoxide poisoning, please know I feel for you! It is a horrific experience in so many ways. The physical symptoms are horrible to live with, the psychological ones even worse, and the total isolation you feel because so few people understand much about carbon monoxide poisoning is possibly the worst part of the whole thing. If you do not feel able to handle this on your own, then remember there is no shame in finding a suitable person to talk to! Talking to a supportive, caring friend or relative, your pastor or a counselor could benefit you greatly. If you opt to speak with a counselor, find someone experienced in treating people who have been through trauma. It may take talking to a few counselors before you find one you are comfortable with, but a good counselor is well worth the effort!

Chapter Twenty Four - Triggers

Triggers are anything that makes you re-experience some feelings from your past. Good triggers are a wonderful thing, such as the smell of lily of the valley that reminds you of your favorite aunt who always wore lily of the valley scented perfume. That scent probably makes you feel content and comfortable, remembering someone special to you.

Unfortunately though, there are also bad triggers. Many of us raised by narcissistic parents know them well, even if we never put a name to them before. For me, being around anyone who is arguing, even if it is only on social media, triggers a lot of anxiety in me. The reason being, when I was growing up and my parents would argue, they would argue in front of me often, sometimes even dragging me into the middle of their argument. They often would complain to me about the other one or ask me to talk to the other one on their behalf. They still do this sometimes even though I am an adult. It was incredibly stressful for me as a child, and not much less stressful as an adult.

Bad triggers can result in emotional flashbacks, which is when you feel overwhelmed by those feelings. This is not a fun place to be, especially if the event made you feel shame. For some reason, shame seems to be the hardest emotional flashback to cope with, at least it is for me.

Once, I posted a picture on Facebook of something I liked and thought was very pretty. Immediately, two people jumped on this, telling me how ugly it was and shaming me for liking it. It made me feel so bad about myself, wondering what was wrong with me, which is how I felt as a child and my mother would criticize something I liked. Ashamed of having my own likes and dislikes. Thankfully, I have some pretty awesome friends. One of those awesome friends defended me vehemently. Since she also liked what I did and defended me so passionately, it helped me to realize there is nothing wrong with me for liking what I did. It was just different than what the other two people would like. That does not automatically make them right and me wrong - it simply makes us different. Realizing this helped the emotional flashback to stop.

When emotional flashbacks happen, you need to relax. Stop what you are doing, and breathe deeply a few times. Tell yourself that this is only an emotional flashback, it cannot hurt you and you are safe. I also recommend asking God to tell you the truth about your situation, then listen quietly for His response.

This may also be a good time to get to the root of this feeling. Why not take the opportunity to make your pain count for something? Ask God what is the root of me feeling the way I do? Chances are, something from a long time ago will pop into your mind. Pay attention to whatever it is. Ask God to help you heal from that painful incident. Tell Him exactly how it made you feel, and let Him comfort and heal you. If He tells you to do something to help yourself heal, then by all means, do it!

Triggers also may trigger an actual flashback, which is the feeling that you are reliving a traumatic event. Flashbacks are a very strange experience because although logically you know you are not in that traumatic situation, you still feel as if you are. It can be very difficult, sometimes impossible, to tell reality from the flashback. Your body responds as if you are physically in the situation once again, not only remembering it. You feel the anxiety, fear, pain and hurt in your mind, while your body experiences a rapid heartbeat, elevated blood pressure, lightheadedness sometimes even aches or pains that happened at the time of the traumatic event although physically you are fine.

Flashbacks require a bit more effort to deal with than emotional flashbacks due to the fact you feel you are actually reliving the traumatic event rather than only feeling the awful feelings of the traumatic event. To deal with them properly, you must learn what grounding techniques work best for you.

Grounding is the act of making sure you know what is real. It need not be as difficult as it may sound. A strong scent or texture can do wonders, as can a strong tasting food or drink. Something that will deeply affect your senses is best, as the sudden "attack" on your senses will force your focus on that sense that is being affected. Once while riding with my husband, I had a flashback. The seats in his truck are a very coarse, scratchy material, so rubbing the fabric helped to keep me grounded. Since then, I have devised a flashback kit I keep handy at all times. In it, I have a very smooth pink quartz rock that is beautiful to look at as well as touch, and two small vials (think of the sample size perfume vials) with two different but strong scents in them. One contains lavender scented oil (lavender is used in aromatherapy for promoting relaxation) and the other is a perfume that my grandmom gave me when I was a little girl. It is a lovely but strong scent, which takes me back to spending time with her when I was a child. Time with her was a very happy time for me as she was one of my favorite people. She is a part of some of my favorite memories growing up.

Other common grounding techniques may involve clapping loudly or stomping hard on the floor. Some people swear by holding an ice cube or wrapping themselves in an extremely soft afghan, blanket or sweater. Tasting something with a very strong flavor can help too, as can loud music. Anything that involves your senses in a bold way possibly can help you to stay grounded.

Do not be surprised if after either a flashback or an emotional flashback if you are very tired, or feel very sensitive, almost emotionally raw for a short period of time. This usually happens to me, and I believe it to be totally normal after such an emotionally draining experience.

Unfortunately triggers cannot be completely avoided, unless you decide to move into a cave, away from civilization completely. The best thing you can do about them is to learn to manage emotional flashbacks or flashbacks if they happen, and remind yourself of exactly what is happening. While yes, it is a very bad memory, it cannot hurt you. You are safe.

Chapter Twenty Five - Complex Post Traumatic Stress Disorder

Complex Post Traumatic Stress Disorder, also known as C-PTSD, is closely related to Post Traumatic Stress Disorder. The primary difference is C-PTSD comes about by repeated traumatic events as opposed to one traumatic event. For example, a rape victim or someone who was in a terrible car accident may develop PTSD but a prisoner of war or abused child will develop C-PTSD.

Many survivors of narcissistic abuse, especially at the hands of their parents, develop the awful symptoms of C-PTSD.

C-PTSD, like PTSD, is an actual brain injury that comes about due to repeated exposure to trauma. Four parts of the brain are injured in cases of PTSD and C-PTSD:

- The prefrontal cortex. This is where emotional regulation and fear responses happen. It does not function properly, which can result in creating hyper-vigilance. Hyper-vigilance is an extreme awareness of one's

surroundings, on the look out for any possible danger.
- The amygdala. Also responsible for regulating emotions. It often enlarges after being overly active for so long, which makes it difficult to control emotions. This can create mood swings that are difficult and sometimes impossible to control.
- The prefrontal lobe. This part of the brain is responsible for language. When it is damaged, it makes it hard to find the right words when you are trying to express your thoughts either in writing or in speaking.
- The hippocampus. This is responsible for memory and understanding experiences. It can shrink after trauma, resulting in poor short term memory.

Symptoms of C-PTSD can include:

- **Depression.** Constantly feeling sad.
- **Anxiety.** Often including panic attacks.
- **Social anxiety or agoraphobia.** Sometimes the anxiety around other people gets so bad, you are afraid to leave your home.
- **Hyper-vigilance.** A fanatical awareness of one's surroundings as well as the body language, tone of voice, reactions and feelings of others to detect any possibility of being hurt.

- **Mood swings and difficulty regulating moods.** Moods change easily and quickly, sometimes beyond one's control.
- **Nightmares.** Both about the traumatic events and about other things that can be upsetting.
- **Sleep troubles.** Trouble falling and staying asleep.
- **Flashbacks.** Feeling as if you are reliving the traumatic event.
- **Emotional flashbacks.** Slightly different than flashbacks, emotional flashbacks make you feel all of the emotions of when you went through the traumatic event, but you are well aware that you are not re-experiencing it.
- **Intrusive thoughts.** Thinking about the traumatic events even when you do not want to. The thoughts seem to just show up whenever they please.
- **Dissociation.** "Spacing out," feeling disconnected to your body.
- **Repressed memories/amnesia.** Forgetting something traumatic until a time when something triggers the memory, bringing it back to the forefront of your mind. It is a common survival skill for traumatized people.
- **Rage.** Turned outward (being abusive or violent to others) or turned inward (eating disorders, addiction, self-destructive behaviors).
- **Low self-esteem.** Possibly even to the point of self-hatred.

- **Belief that one has no control over a situation, even when they do.**
- **Avoidance.** Withdrawing from relationships in an attempt to protect oneself from being hurt.
- **Fear of abandonment.** A constant fear of those you love leaving you, even when the fear is unfounded.
- **Difficulty concentrating.** Having trouble focusing.
- **Short term memory problems.** Being able to remember something from twenty years ago, but having trouble remembering why you entered a room two minutes ago.
- **Being pessimistic.** Always seeing the worst possible scenario in any situation. Exaggerating how bad a situation is, even minor situations.
- **Being cynical and untrusting.**
- **Feeling hopeless.**
- **Constant fatigue.** When the mind is under stress, the body feels it. With C-PTSD, the mind is constantly under a great deal of stress, which constantly tires the body.
- **Physical problems.** Inflammatory disorders such as arthritis or irritable bowel disease are especially common. Digestive issues are as well. Aches and pains with no known physical cause happen often. High blood pressure and fibromyalgia are fairly common as well. I also have experienced old, healed

injuries suddenly begin to ache again when the C-PTSD flares up, such as after a flashback.

    Everyone is different, so everyone's experiences with C-PTSD are also different. You may experience only a couple of the symptoms above, or all of them. Some may come and go while others seem to be a permanent fixture. In my experience, I have had many symptoms at once, but as of this particular moment, I am barely having any. That however, is subject to change at any time. I will not complain though, because even if the good days do not last long, at least they happen. I could not handle having constant, very bad days. Good days are a blessing and a wonderful reprieve, something never to take for granted.
    Treating C-PTSD is not an easy task. Many counselors are not equipped to deal with this disorder, so finding one who is may be a daunting task. It may take visiting several counselors before you find one you are comfortable with.

Chapter Twenty Six - Trauma Changes You

I have been through many traumas in my life. I grew up with narcissistic abuse, my ex husband was a narcissist, have experienced loss of friendships and loved ones, had several pretty serious nervous breakdowns since my first one at age nineteen, and have come very close to death. I can tell you from experience that trauma truly changes you, and sometimes in very unique ways.

Thankfully, the changes are not always a bad thing. After coming close to dying from carbon monoxide poisoning last February, I did a great deal of soul searching once I got home from the hospital. I quickly realized that I needed to make changes in my life. My anxiety levels were so bad just prior to getting sick that I actually had lost quite a bit of hair. It suddenly became very brittle and fragile instead of strong and healthy as it always had been. I decided I had to try to get a better handle on anxiety, and could not let this continue to happen. If this was happening to my hair, what other damage was happening to the inside of my body?

I stopped worrying so much about things I had no control over by reminding myself I had no control over such things. I also stopped judging and criticizing myself for having C-PTSD. Once I started to feel a little better, I started doing things I had wanted to try but had been afraid to try, such as working with clay. I began doing nice little things for myself on a regular basis. I also became much less afraid of confronting bad behaviors when people were mistreating me. I realized life is just too short and can end too suddenly and unexpectedly. There is no reason to tolerate abuse and waste time with that.

All of those changes are very good things, and I am quite happy with them.

The changes can be a bad thing sometimes, too, however. Many victims of narcissistic abuse have C-PTSD. Many others have become bitter and untrusting of people due to the pain they have experienced. Others end up with an unhealthy addiction such as drugs, alcohol, or food or they abuse other people.

Whether the changes that have happened to you are good or bad, I encourage you to look closely at the changes. Accept that they have happened and why. For the good changes, embrace them and appreciate them. Thank God that some good came out of the awful things you have been through.

If you cannot find anything good, then ask God to show you. Romans 8:28 says, **"And we know that all things work together for good to them that love God, to them who are the called according to his purpose." (KJV)** While I know it seems like nothing good could possibly come out of narcissistic abuse, it really can. Many people have found an inner strength they never knew they had. They also have an incredible amount of empathy, because they know how badly it feels to hurt. They have the ability to read people well, and can tell if someone is being genuine, honest or deceptive. They also have a healthy perspective that only comes about by experiencing trauma. People who have not been through many hardships worry easily over trivial things. People who have been through some hardships or trauma know that the little things are not worth worrying about, and refuse to do it. Many people also use their pain to help others. If they were abused, they speak out against abuse or teach others about what they can do if they are being abused. Another interesting change that often occurs as a result of trauma is a sudden inability to tolerate abuse or nonsense. I have learned that the more I heal, the less able I am to tolerate it quietly when someone is deliberately abusive or even insensitive to me. I am not unreasonable about it. I understand everyone has a bad day sometimes, and sometimes they act rude, hurtful or insensitive in a moment of anger or frustration. However, when it is obvious someone is purposely being cruel to me, it angers me badly. I used to take abuse in stride, assuming on some level I deserve nothing better, but no longer. Now that person will be called out on their bad behavior instead of me letting it slide, and holding the anger in.

Please do not think that I am saying that because something good came from being abused by a narcissist, that you need to be grateful for the abuse you endured. I am not saying that at all. I seriously doubt any human being ever could be grateful for experiencing such horrific pain as the kind of pain that comes from narcissistic abuse. Instead, I am saying that finding some good in the bad can help you. Knowing your pain was not for nothing is very helpful. When you feel as if your pain had no purpose, it is possibly the most depressing feeling in the world. That is what I am trying to spare you from.

As for the bad changes, it is normal, I think, to beat yourself up over them. After all, narcissists beat us up for every flaw we have (whether the flaw is real or a figment of their imagination) so much that we learn to do the same thing to ourselves even if they are not around. However, it does no good. In fact, it will do more harm than good, as it will damage your self-esteem. Instead, why not try to look at the problems as a normal result of an abnormal situation? No one escapes narcissistic abuse intact. It is only normal that you would have some problems stemming from it.

You will need to deal with the bad things. If you opt to get into counseling to do this, be sure to find a counselor who understands trauma and narcissistic abuse. This may not be easy, and you may need to talk to a few counselors before finding the right one.

Another aspect of trauma changing you that I have noticed is I change often now. The person I was last year is not the same person I am now. I really am not sure why this happens. Being someone who never has been a big fan of change, I found it very unsettling for a while. However, I finally decided if it is going to happen anyway, I might as well just accept it and go with the flow. Instead of being annoyed at myself for my changing likes and dislikes periodically, I take the time to get to know the new me without judgment. The good thing is it turns out that I am pretty interesting. I am sure you will find this same thing out about yourself.

Chapter Twenty Seven - Dreams

I always have had very vivid dreams and plenty of equally vivid nightmares. However, the more I began to heal from the narcissistic abuse I experienced, the more nightmares I began to have and the more bizarre they and my dreams became.

Once I developed C-PTSD, I read that one of the symptoms is nightmares. The little I read about that at that time said that the nightmares were about reliving painful, abusive episodes. I rarely had nightmares like that. Instead, my nightmares were of entirely different things, such as witnessing an airplane crash, car wrecks, seeing murder victims or buildings on fire. My non-nightmare dreams became more peculiar as well, such as dreaming of traveling alone (I am not a fan of traveling, especially alone) or being in a hospital, usually visiting someone rather than being admitted.

Honestly, it was rather scary at first, wondering what these dreams meant. Why did I not relive the terrible experiences I have been through in my nightmares like normal people with C-PTSD? Was something wrong with me? Were things not as bad as I thought they were? And really, what was with the nightly just plain weird dreams? I began to pray about my questions, and God showed me many interesting things about dreams

God will send messages to you via your dreams, so it is very important to pay attention to them. He always has done it, and this is mentioned quite a few times in the Bible. Here are a few examples for your consideration:

- *Genesis 46:2 "God spoke to unto Israel in the visions of the night and said, "Jacob, Jacob." And he said, "Here am I."" (KJV)*
- *Daniel 2:19 "Then was the secret revealed unto Daniel in a night vision. Then Daniel blessed the God of heaven." (KJV)*
- *Daniel 2:28 "But there is a God in heaven that revealeth secrets, and maketh known to the king Nebuchadnezzar what shall be in the latter days. Thy dream, and the visions of thy head upon thy bed, are these;" (KJV)*

I have started to write down my dreams along with their meaning. It is handy to have this reference sometimes. You can learn a great deal about your mental health by understanding your dreams.

To figure out the interpretation, I use a website that explains the symbolic meaning of things you see in your dreams. I look up everything I can remember in the dream, even down to colors sometimes, writing it all down, reading over it and once I am finished all of that, I pray, asking God to help me understand His message in the dream. God then helps me to make sense of the dream. Sometimes, I do not even need to do this as He shows me the interpretation as soon as I wake up or think about the dream, but that is quite rare.

C-PTSD is a very individual disorder. No two people with it share exactly the same symptoms or do the symptoms manifest the same way. Dreams are no different. Many people do relive the trauma in their nightmares, but many others do not. Some people are like me, and only sometimes relive trauma in their nightmares. Often their nightmares are of totally unrelated topics.

Even if you do not have C-PTSD, God showed me that processing trauma is a very individual experience. Much like those with C-PTSD, some people who have experienced trauma relive it in their nightmares while others do not. Some have odd nightmares like I do instead of reliving the trauma nightly. No two people process trauma exactly the same way.

God also showed me that your brain is constantly processing whatever it experiences, trying to make sense of the things that happen whether those things are good, bad or indifferent. Dreams manifest that many times.

Part of your brain's constant effort to process things may result in not remembering your dreams. I used to remember most of mine until I got C-PTSD. There are often nights now when I know I dreamed, I remember dreaming but I cannot remember what the dreams were about. That is simply the brain trying to process something, and it is not important that you remember it. If it was, God would have let you remember it. During those times I really wonder if it is my brain still trying to make sense of the many traumatic experiences I have been through in my life.

Dreams are always about the dreamer. Even if you dream of other people, there is a meaning in there about you, not them. Maybe you need to be more or less like the person you are dreaming about. I urge you to pray about it when you dream of other people.

Dreams are also symbolic. For example, if you need to take more control over your life and stop allowing others to push you around, you will not dream that someone tells you that fact. Instead, you may often dream about cars, yours specifically. Cars symbolize your life. If you are driving your car, you are in control. If someone else is driving your car, that person has too much power over you. If you dream you are in the backseat of your car while another person is driving, you are much too passive in your own life.

    Dreams are utterly fascinating to me. They are also so educational. I would like to encourage you to find a good dream dictionary or dream website, and begin to interpret your dreams. Pray about them too, and God will show you what they mean.

Chapter Twenty Eight - Sickness

Often, narcissists are very healthy people. They rarely get colds, stomach bugs or have serious health problems. They recover quickly, too, on those rare occasions when they are sick.

Those around them, however, tend to get sick much more frequently, and often with more serious illnesses.

The reason for this, I believe, is stress.

Time spent with a narcissist is extremely stressful. The constant walking on eggshells feeling, watching everything you say or do. Always having to think about what you say before you say it in an effort to avoid criticisms or worse yet, the narcissistic rage. Either having to set and enforce your boundaries at every moment or disregarding them in an effort to appease the narcissist. It is exhausting and extremely stressful to be under such constant pressure. The human body is not made to live under so much stress for long periods of time.

Narcissistic abuse can cause many mental and physical illnesses, some of which can potentially be life threatening. Depression, C-PTSD and digestive issues are probably the most well known problems, but there are many other potential problems that can arise from narcissistic abuse.

Addictions, self-harming (such as cutting or pulling out hair) and eating disorders are also very common. It is normal to want to escape the pain of narcissistic abuse, and drowning your pain in cutting yourself, alcohol, drugs, food or sex can numb that pain for a short time. Addictions, self-harming behaviors and eating disorders also can give you a false sense of having some control in your life, which is something you do not have when being abused by a narcissist.

Weight gain is another common problem. When stressed or upset, people tend to make poor food choices. Also, extreme stress can slow your metabolism, which leads to weight gain.

Sleep problems are also very common. Stress of any kind tends to make your mind race, thinking of ways to fix the stressful situation. This can make sleeping difficult, either falling asleep or staying asleep. It also can provide fodder for nightmares when you finally do fall asleep. Poor sleeping habits can lead to irritability, moodiness, achiness and feeling just plain yukky.

Inflammatory disorders are common too, due to elevated levels of the stress hormone cortisol in the body. Arthritis, fibromyalgia, and irritable bowel syndrome are quite common. I have had arthritis since I was thirty, which is much younger than my parents were when they got arthritis.

Stress also can compromise the function of your immune system, so you may find yourself getting infections, colds and other viruses easily. A compromised immune system also can mean wounds heal slower than they should.

Aches and pains with no known cause are extremely common, especially in the lower back. When I was nineteen, during an argument with my mother, she threw me into a wall. I had extreme pain in my lower left back for ten years from that episode, but no doctor ever found a cause for the pain. In fact, only my chiropractor believed I was injured, even though she could see no cause for my suffering. I wonder if the trauma of my mother's attack and believing she wanted to kill me caused that back pain.

Speaking of pain, I often have old injuries begin to hurt again long after they have healed when I feel very stressed, especially if I have to deal with my narcissistic parents. Once I leave their presence, the pain goes away fairly quickly.

Headaches are particularly common in survivors of narcissistic abuse; stress headaches or even migraines. High blood pressure can trigger headaches too, so it is important to get to the cause of your headaches.

High blood pressure, diabetes or low blood sugar levels also are common problems. My blood pressure and glucose levels were at their highest when I have had a great deal of interaction with my parents.

Last December, my father was in the hospital for about one week. It was a very stressful time for me. I had to step far out of my comfort zone by leaving home daily, rearranging my schedule, dealing with doctors and spending quite a bit of time daily with my mother. Plus, my father had some very disturbing reactions to some medications that terrified me. This is when I learned that extreme stress can cause a symptom I never heard of before - brittle hair. I have heard it can cause hair loss, but rather than my hair falling out, it became very brittle and broke easily. My hair was a couple of inches past my shoulders, but the most brittle parts broke off at about two inches long. It was terrifying at first, because I thought only health problems or medications caused such a problem. I was wrong though, as extreme stress can do it too.

Do you have any of the above mentioned problems while the narcissist who abused you is healthy?

Aside from treating whatever health problems you have, it is best to use wisdom on dealing with your narcissist. Only answer her calls when you believe you are able to do so. The same goes for visiting. In fact, I have learned to pray when I see my parents' phone number come up on my caller ID if I have any doubts. God immediately lets me know if I should or should not answer the phone. He also strengthens me to avoid answering it if I am in need of it. I realize that sounds silly, but even after years of not living with my parents, sometimes it is hard for me not to slip into old, dysfunctional habits, like doing whatever they want and ignoring my needs. Answering their calls is something they want, so sometimes it is hard for me to take care of myself by not answering a call from them if I am unable to for any reason. Those times, God helps me by giving me inner strength.

Learning ways to manage your stress levels will help you to feel better as well.

If you have gone no contact yet still experience these health problems, I pray they will improve as you heal as they have with me. The more I heal, the less problems I have and the more easily the ones I do have are managed. I also have learned how to relax better, which helps tremendously.

Chapter Twenty Nine - Bad Days Happen

When healing from narcissistic abuse, there are going to be some bad times. As I have said before, healing is never a simple, uphill battle. It is more like going up a windy, rocky mountain road with a lot of potholes and valleys compared to a level, smooth, straight concrete highway. Some people experience more potholes and valleys than others, but everyone experiences them. That is perfectly normal, although while you are experiencing those times, they probably will not feel normal.

Being subject to narcissistic abuse, especially at the hands of a parent, is incredibly destructive. It damages your perspective, your emotional health and your self-esteem. It also is incredibly hurtful when you realize that your own mother did what she did to you for her own selfish motives, and did not care how badly she hurt you. In fact, she hurt you deliberately just to amuse herself sometimes. How painful it is to learn that!

It is only natural that some days you will feel strong and your healing is going well, while other days you cry and are angry about what you have been through and why those things were done to you. I have been focusing on healing since 2000, and still have some days when I get very angry or sad or both when I think about what I have been through. Granted, those days have decreased greatly over the years, but they still happen once in a while. I honestly wonder if they ever will stop completely.

Those days are simply stumbling blocks. While they may feel at the time as if they are devastating setbacks, truly they are not. They only make you stumble for a short time.

When stumbling blocks happen, you need to do some things to handle them in a healthy manner. First, you need to accept them. They are going to happen no matter what you do. Do not fight them. Like I said, they are a natural part of the healing process.

Second, deal with the emotions you feel. Are you angry? Why? Get that anger out. I have found either talking to God about it or journaling about it to be very helpful. Some people swear by the chair technique, where they pretend their abuser is sitting in an empty chair, then telling that chair exactly what they feel. Others write letters they never send. I have done that too, then burned the letters. Talk to someone non-judgmental and supportive. Beating up pillows can be a good way to get the anger out of you too.

If you are not angry, but hurt, the same thing still goes - get that hurt out of you! Cry, talk to God, talk to a supportive friend or relative or write in your journal.

Lastly, be gentle with yourself. Let yourself feel what you feel, and do whatever it is you need to do without judgment or criticism. Take care of yourself. Do nurturing things that make you feel good. Indulge in your favorite movies while in your pajamas and eating chocolate. (While I do not encourage emotional eating, sometimes you just need to splurge a little, and it is fine!) Get a manicure and pedicure in some fun color that you normally do not wear, such as neon pink. Rather than cook dinner, pick up something you really enjoy. Spend the day in bed with a good book and some herbal tea.

Chapter Thirty - Narcissistic Abuse Changes All Of Your Relationships

A particularly painful aspect of surviving a narcissistic parent is when you start to see what is happening, and talking about it, people will abandon you. Many people do NOT like unpleasant subject matters, and will go to great lengths to avoid them. People with debilitating health problems know this all too well – they often lose friends and family after receiving a diagnosis of a dreadful disease. The people who once were closest to them suddenly have no time for them any longer, or accuse them of faking the illness for attention, so they do not have to work, so they can get pain medication, or other outrageous reasons.

Something similar to this situation is also very common with adult children of narcissistic parents. They are accused of seeking attention, being overly dramatic, living in the past and many other awful and untrue things.

It has happened in my life many times. My first boyfriend (now ex-husband) pointed out to me when we were seventeen that my mother's behavior was controlling and abnormal. I had told myself she was overprotective all my life, but quickly saw he was right. There was no more denying it anymore, because she changed so drastically when I said I wanted to start dating at seventeen. She suddenly began to scream at me daily, accuse me of doing terrible things I was not doing (drugs, having sex with the entire high school football team, etc.), and even had someone at my school report back to her nightly on what I had done during my day at school. I began to talk to a few people about the abuse I was enduring at home, and then my circle of friends became smaller. Ones that stayed were obviously very uncomfortable with the topic, often changing the subject as soon as I started talking. One counselor even refused to treat me any longer after meeting my mother. She said I was a bad daughter, and she refused to treat me any longer because of it. I talked very little about my experiences after that until many years later, once I started learning about narcissism. Then, I began to talk more and also to write about it. While my writing career suddenly began to take off, my personal relationships changed, especially when I also admitted to having Complex Post Traumatic Stress Disorder, also known as C-PTSD. A few of my relationships became closer, especially with those who also survived a narcissistic upbringing, but many did not. Some people who I once thought were caring, safe people suddenly became very judgmental, telling me how I needed to just get over it, let it go, forgive and forget, stop living in the past, I use having C-PTSD to get attention and even how I needed to be the one to fix things in my relationship with my parents.

These episodes hurt badly, and made me so angry! It is not fair nor is it right to be mistreated as a result of how someone else has treated you! That simply makes no sense! I also began to feel like I did as a child – like everything that was wrong in the relationship with my parents was all my fault, I should fix it and if I did not do so, I was a failure. Not a nice way to feel at all!

I also realized that when people treated me this way, my feelings towards them sometimes just died suddenly. I think this can happen when the relationship is especially important to you, if you are very close to the person who says such hurtful things, because you feel so incredibly betrayed. You thought this person was the last person on Earth who would hurt you so badly, then they do it. You are shocked and deeply wounded by their actions.

    I experienced this with someone I loved dearly. She could be rather blunt with her words, and a couple of times over the years, her bluntness really hurt me. She never had said anything about my relationship with my parents though, probably because she knew very little about it. I never had the urge to share much on that topic with her. We were emailing back and forth one day, and she said something about the terrible mood swings she had during peri-menopause. She said I should watch out for them. I said thanks to my mental health problems, I am so used to them that should not really be an issue for me. She wrote back, saying, "I say this in love, but you really need to get over your childhood hurts. We all have them. I had them too, but I got over them. You need to let go of the past." It blew me away. I did not expect a comment on my childhood at all, let alone something so cruel. I was so hurt, I could not even respond to that email until the following day. The comment just came out of the blue, and was so invalidating. "Childhood hurts"?! No, what I experienced at the hands of my parents was not "childhood hurts." It was abuse, plain and simple. And to this day, my parents are still abusive, which is why I have only limited contact with them. This person obviously did not understand any of that, however. When I calmed down enough, I wrote her back. I told her I mean no disrespect, but I was not asking for your thoughts on my mental health, then changed the topic of our conversation. She did not speak to me for months after that, and during that time, the love I once had felt for her died. I was not angry, I wished her no harm, but suddenly I felt nothing at all for her. When she died a couple of years later, I barely cried. I felt nothing other than sadness at how things changed so drastically in our relationship.

If you too have experienced similar losses of relationships and invalidation, you are not alone! I understand your pain and frustration all too well.

Unfortunately, I do not think there is any way to completely avoid such situations. The simple fact is that so many people do not like unpleasant subject matters. They prefer light, fluffy, happy things, as the unpleasant things make them uncomfortable. Many people also cannot handle discussing unpleasant things about the parent/child relationship. They may come from a good home, and cannot comprehend that any parent would abuse a child, or maybe they came from a dysfunctional home, and you discussing your own painful experiences trigger feelings they simply are not ready to deal with yet. Others may feel uncomfortable when you talk about your experiences for other unknown reasons. Whatever the reason, however, **no one has the right to invalidate your pain!**

To deal with the pain you feel when this happens, please try to keep the last paragraph in mind. In spite of how it feels, most people really are not trying to hurt you by what they say or do - they simply have their own issues, or are even convinced that they are helping you when they give you advice, as poor as that advice may be.

Also, acknowledge your feelings. Just because others are offended somehow by your feelings does not mean you need to ignore those feelings. It only means you need to avoid discussing those feelings with those particular people. You are hurt and/or angry, and that is OK, no matter what anyone says. Cry, talk to someone safe, journal, pray, but acknowledge your feelings and get them out somehow. Feelings are a natural part of life - respect them, and do not ignore them. Ignoring only leads to very bad things like depression and physical health problems.

You also need to be aware that part of the reason that being invalidated upsets you so much is because it triggers old feelings that you experienced at the hand of your narcissistic mother. Narcissists demand that their abuse be kept secret, so when someone else wants to silence you years later, guilt for "tattling" may suddenly appear. Or, invalidating your pain makes you feel as you did when your mother did it to you as a child - like you are not allowed to have feelings, because they are only a nuisance to others. I am not saying that these triggers mean you are overreacting to being invalidated, of course. I am saying that those triggers may make you less able to realize at first that you are not wrong for discussing this topic. Triggers can get you caught up in your feelings and unable to see the truth of the situation at hand. Being aware of your triggers helps to see the truth of the situation at hand easier.

Be good to yourself after someone has hurt you. Once you get a firm grasp on your feelings and triggers, do little nice things for yourself. Take a bubble bath, read a good book, drink some herbal tea, or do some other things that make you feel good.

And, ask God to help you let go of the hurt, anger and frustration you feel. You deserve better than to carry around those negative feelings. Besides, you have too much already to deal with considering you are recovering from growing up with a narcissistic mother. That needs your attention much more, so you can heal.

Also, it may be a good idea to ask God to help you to evaluate this relationship. A person who invalidates you in one area may do it in other areas, which means this person is not good for you. It may be time to end the relationship.

If you feel you need safe emotional support and are not finding it with friends or family, there are other options. Counseling would be a good option, provided you can find a counselor who understands narcissism and narcissistic abuse. It may take seeing a few counselors before you find one who meets this criterion and is someone you feel comfortable with.

There are many, many websites and blogs available where people share their stories online. Reading through them may help you to feel less alone. Also, when others explain what they feel or are struggling with as a result of narcissistic abuse, it may help you to understand your own struggles better.

There are also a great many online forums where you can anonymously discuss your situation. I have a small forum plus a Facebook group. (Links to both are on my website at www.CynthiaBaileyRug.com. Check them out if you like. I would love to have you be a part of one or both!) There are many, many more forums both online and on Facebook besides mine. Undoubtedly you can find one that you like. I do urge you to be cautious with such groups, however. Sometimes, the people in them can be rather cliquish. Also, sometimes narcissists will join these groups and cause a great deal of pain and discord among the other members. I have seen it happen. Being online rather than in person, narcissists can be hard to spot at first. They may appear as victims, but it will not take long before their masks come off. They will start to give advice no one asked for or being judgmental. They may offer subtle criticisms. They may preach one answer for everyone, such as going no contact. These are all warning signs of a potential narcissist in the group.

Chapter Thirty One - You Are The Black Sheep Of Your Family

Anyone who speaks openly about narcissistic abuse automatically becomes the black sheep of their family, but especially adult children of narcissistic parents. They are often told to stop living in the past, get over it, they are too negative for discussing this topic, that it never happened or other very hurtful, invalidating things by the very people they expect to be there for them. The experience is almost as painful as the narcissistic abuse.

Jesus was familiar with this type of phenomenon. Mark 6 tells the story of a time when Jesus went home and preached. Those who knew him were offended at His preaching, not believing in what He said. As a result, He did no miracles in the town. In Mark 6:4, Jesus says, *"But Jesus said to them, A prophet is not without honor (deference, reverence) except in his [own] country and among [his] relatives and in his [own] house." (AMP)* This verse struck me as especially fascinating one day. I realized it is just how people are. They often will have respect for total strangers above their own family. Those who knew Jesus were no exception.

People seem to have a set of expectations of others, but especially those in their own family. When someone steps outside of those expectations and talks about or does something rather radical, it makes others uncomfortable. In Jesus' situation, He went from a carpenter to preaching the Gospel. Talk about a radical change! People were uncomfortable enough with the Gospel, but to hear it preached by their carpenter, their brother or neighbor? It was too far from their expectations of Him for them to be comfortable accepting what he had to say.

Speaking out about the narcissistic abuse you have experienced is much the same way. Your narcissist has told people close to you all about you. Your failures and short comings in particular. They also have seen the way you behave around her. Her words and your once dysfunctional behavior helped develop their opinion and expectations of you. They will not expect you to be one who speaks out against abuse.

They believe that you are stupid, overly dramatic, dishonest, etc. as the narcissist who abused you said you were. (Narcissists are very adept at convincing people of what they say, after all, so it is understandable people believe her.) They do not think they should believe anything you have to say because of that.

People also do not want to hear about abuse. It is a very unpleasant subject, and most people prefer only discussing lighter topics. Some people close to you may feel guilty for not trying to stop the abuse, and you talking about it makes them feel bad. Their solution is to try to shut you up rather than admitting how they feel, or apologizing for letting you down. Still others may have been similarly abused, and you being open about your situation triggers their own unpleasant memories that they are unwilling to face. Others may be of the school of thought that abuse is not something "nice" people talk about. There are also those, primarily naïve Christians, of the "forgive and forget" mentality who believe if you would simply forgive and forget your painful experiences, everything would be completely fine.

Any of these situations can be incredibly painful and frustrating, especially since even if you no longer discuss the abuse with these people, a wedge in the relationship will remain in place.

The only way I have found to deal with this is to stop discussing your experiences with your family members unless you have absolutely no doubt that they are incredibly supportive of you no matter what. Be sure to pray as well, asking God to give you discernment. This is not fool proof though, and sometimes you may be painfully surprised at who turns on you.

It usually is best to speak about your experiences with narcissistic abuse with those who are not as close to you. Friends and even strangers on forums can be much more validating and comforting than family when it comes to this topic of narcissistic abuse. My Facebook group has been so much more supportive of me than some of the people who are closest to me. Other members in the group have said the same thing about my group. I strongly recommend looking for an online support group as a safe place to discuss your experiences, as I mentioned in the previous chapter. Just be sure to sit back quietly and watch how the members interact for a while before you speak out. Also as I previously mentioned, some groups can be rather "cliquey" and some have narcissists in them. It will not take you long to figure out if a group is right for you if you simply observe its members for a short while.

Chapter Thirty Two - Dating Or Marrying A Narcissist

A very common phenomenon I have noticed is that once you have been abused by a narcissist, especially a parent, you seem to attract them. Either as friends or romantic interests, they seem to keep showing up everywhere. And inevitably, in many cases, the victim marries one of them.

I am no exception. My ex husband was very narcissistic. He was very much like my narcissistic mother. He wanted me to look, dress and act a certain way. He also ignored my feelings on these matters, and really all matters. Everything was about him in our marriage, what he wanted, thought, or felt. I think the fact that he and my mother were so much alike is why they hated each other so much. They were too much alike. There is also the fact that they both thought they had the right to mold me into whatever it was that they wanted me to be, so it was a battle for control between the two of them when he came into my life.

When I eventually realized how similar to my mother my ex husband was, I wondered how I could be so stupid. I had gotten out of my parents' home only seven months before marrying my ex. I wanted peace and a happy life for once, to share my life with someone who loved me. How could I think I would get any of that with someone like this?!

Looking back, I think I understand now why I got involved with him, and so many other victims of narcissistic abuse have gotten involved with narcissists, too. It truly has nothing to do with your intelligence at all. In fact, my IQ is 138, which is near genius.

Growing up with a narcissistic parent, you get a really skewed view of love because of how she treats you. You think love equals criticism, screaming, being mocked and invalidated. You do not realize that genuine love involves nothing of the sort. You mistakenly think people who treat you the way your narcissistic mother did love you. You tend to avoid those who treat you gently and lovingly, because you do not trust their foreign ways.

Even if you did not have a narcissistic parent, but a narcissistic lover or spouse, the intense gaslighting may have convinced you that their way of showing you love is the real thing. They are extremely adept at convincing their partners that their abusive behavior is actually loving behavior, and that they only have their partner's best interests at heart.

People also naturally gravitate to what is familiar, whether it is good or bad. If you grew up around narcissism, even though it hurts you, you are attracted to it because, to a degree, it is what you are comfortable with.

Growing up with a narcissistic parent (or two), you are deprived of love and positive attention. A narcissistic lover will pursue you enthusiastically, finally providing that positive attention and love. My ex husband would not take no for an answer when he first asked me out. He finally wore me down. I was tired of his constant pressure, so I risked saying yes, I would go out with him, even though I knew my mother would not approve and I would have to sneak around behind her back to date him. I was seventeen years old, and although I was not attracted to him, that persistence was very flattering. I also was so desperate for love and positive attention, it overrode common sense.

Two years later, he used this same persistence to get me to marry him, even though in my heart, I knew it was a big mistake.

Being deprived of love and positive attention can make you desperate for it. That desperation shows, and people pick up on it. Healthy people are put off by desperation. They want to be with other healthy people. Narcissists, however, are attracted to the desperation. They think it makes you an easy target for them, and often times, they are correct.

If you have fallen into the trap of being with a narcissist, do not beat yourself up for it. Everyone makes mistakes. Plus, if you were raised by narcissistic parents, you practically were groomed for this situation. Your narcissistic parents trained you from the day you were born to be obedient, to be a good victim, to do whatever you are told. It is only natural that you would marry someone who does such things to you.

Narcissists are very cunning, skilled predators. They select their victims very carefully. Not only do they want people who are "good victims", but who are also caring, generous, compassionate and intelligent. They exploit these caring type qualities to gain whatever they want. As for intelligence, that is also good for them. Intelligence means you will learn quickly how to be what they want you to be. It also is a challenge to the narcissist. It makes her feel good about herself if she can tear down an intelligent person.

The good news about this awful phenomenon is that as you heal from narcissistic abuse, narcissists are attracted to you less and less. Emotionally healthy people seldom attract emotionally unhealthy people. As you get healthier, you also learn more about how to set and enforce good boundaries, which is something narcissists cannot abide. They have no tolerance at all for someone who will not put up with their antics, and will move on to another target.

As your self-esteem improves, this too will put off narcissists. Once you realize your worth, and will not let anyone shake it, you become impossible for a narcissist to victimize. They will want nothing to do with you if you cannot be their victim, and they will move onto someone else.

Let's not forget too, that as you heal, obviously you are learning plenty about Narcissistic Personality Disorder. You learn the signs of it, and what they mean. Not only does this help you to heal, it also helps you to learn to spot a narcissist a mile away. You will become good at avoiding them because you can spot them so easily. And, if somehow you miss the early warning signs and end up dealing with a narcissist, you will know good, effective ways to deal with her. Ways that, chances are, will make her want to get far away from you and as quickly as possible.

Chapter Thirty Three - The Good Things

Believe it or not, some good things come from narcissistic abuse that you may not have noticed. It can be easy to overlook them and get caught up in all the bad.

You develop a grateful heart. After being through so much trauma and pain, you truly appreciate anything and everything that does not cause you pain but instead blesses you. One thing I have learned to appreciate, especially lately, is comfort. Not that I wear sweatpants wherever I am, but I make sure that my clothing is always comfortable as well as pretty, whether it is dressy or casual. I also like to be in a comfortable environment. My bedroom is my favorite place in the world, and I spend a lot of time in there, not only when I am sleeping.

You also know how to love. In spite of having no good example of how to love from your narcissistic parents, you know how to love unconditionally. Having such a bad example of love somehow taught you how to love in a good, healthy way.

You have great empathy. You understand what it is like to be invalidated and rejected, so you refuse to do that to others. Instead, you offer others love, support and caring.

You are strong. Surviving a narcissist makes you incredibly strong. You have to be strong in order to survive with your sanity in tact!

I would like to encourage you to focus on these things about yourself. Appreciate those good qualities you have. Granted, doing so will not make you grateful for the horrible abuse you experienced, nothing can make that happen, but at least you will see some good things came out of it. It truly is beneficial when you can realize that some good came from something bad. It comforts you to know that your pain counted for something.

Romans 8:28 "And we know that all things work together for good to them that love God, to them who are the called according to his purpose." (KJV)

Chapter Thirty Four - What Now?

Now that you understand that so many issues you are currently facing stem from narcissistic abuse, you are probably wondering what to do from here.

I always recommend focusing often on your healing. Narcissistic abuse victims have been through a tremendous amount of pain and suffering. It truly seeps into every aspect of your being, so healing will not happen quickly. I firmly believe it to be a life long effort, but even so, keep plugging away the best you can. It is worth the effort as you watch yourself become free little by little of the nasty effects of narcissistic abuse!

While you need to focus on your healing, you also need to take breaks from it as well, as I mentioned in the chapter entitled, "Preparing To Heal." There needs to be balance so you do not get mired down in the darkness of it all. Sometimes, you can become depressed, because when healing, there are times you will think about what you have been through too much, how much you think is wrong with you, or even how far you feel you have to go to be healed. It also can be very easy to become overwhelmed. It often happens where you look at how far you have to go to be healed, rather than how far you have come. That can be so overwhelming as well as discouraging. So rather than depress or discourage yourself or get overwhelmed, take some time out deliberately not to focus on healing or any aspect of what you have been through. Do it often. And, when you do, focus on something more positive and lighter. Participate in a hobby you enjoy like drawing, crocheting, painting or puzzles. Maybe read a novel on light subject matter. Call a close friend and share some laughs. Go to lunch and shopping with some friends.

Learn about self-care, and practice it often. What can you do for yourself that makes you feel nurtured? Nurturing actions are like a salve to the soul. They soothe you when you are hurting. Even if you are not hurting, nurture yourself anyway. Nurturing actions say, "I love you. I care about you. I want you to feel loved." Doing such things for yourself not only helps you to feel better, it is good for your self-esteem.

Learn as much as you possibly can about narcissism. Learning about this evil disorder is extremely helpful when you have to deal with narcissists in many ways. You will recognize immediately when she starts trying to gaslight you. You know that what she is doing to you is not about you, even though it may feel like it at the time. The hurtful actions are all about the narcissist and her insecurities. She is accusing you of awful things because she is projecting her flaws onto you so she can get mad about those flaws without admitting she has them. Or, she is trying to hurt you because somehow it makes her feel better about herself to have that kind of effect over another person. Knowing it is not personal helps you not to be so upset when bad things happen.

Knowing about narcissism also helps you to know what to expect from narcissists. You know that if you are critical, you can expect to be on the receiving end of a narcissistic rage. Or, you know if you provide that precious narcissistic supply, she will want to spend an inordinate amount of time with you, draining you dry emotionally.

A good education about Narcissistic Personality Disorder is a very valuable tool to help you when you have to deal with these people.

Learn to celebrate your victories, big or small. I have the bad habit of looking more at how far I have to go instead of how far I have come, and it is extremely discouraging! Unfortunately I think it is also a pretty typical thing for most people to do, especially those subjected to narcissistic abuse. We have heard do so often about all of our flaws that we learned to automatically look at them before looking at the good things, if we even look at the good at all. It is time to change that old, bad habit, and start not only looking at what you have accomplished, but celebrating them as well. By celebrating, I am not necessarily saying take a cruise because you finally told your narcissistic mother no. If you want to do that and can afford it, great! Go for it! If you prefer a smaller scale celebration, however, you can do what I have learned to do. Simply take a few moments to bask in the positive of what just happened. For example, only recently I have begun to ignore my parents' guilt trips or attempts to pry information from me. When these things happen, I used to feel guilty, or answer fully any questions about me they had. Now, I completely ignore what they are doing, which clearly annoys them but also it makes them stop when they realize their actions are not gaining them the desired results. This is a victory as far as I am concerned, and one I celebrate each time it happens. Each celebration involves me simply taking a few moments to tell myself that I did a good job and handled the situation very well. It is not easy breaking old, lifelong habits of being hyper-critical of myself, but I have done it. I am getting healthier and stronger, and should be proud of this. Sometimes too I reward myself with a little prize. A small milkshake, a new purse (I love purses) or some random little prize from one of the local thrift stores I like will suffice. It usually is nothing big, but is something I enjoy and that makes me smile.

Pay close attention to your dreams also. As I mentioned in chapter twenty seven entitled "Dreams," God often speaks to people in dreams. Dreams can teach you a great deal about where you are in your healing journey. They can show you a great deal about yourself.

Another wise thing for you to do as you heal is to teach your children, if you have them, what you are learning, as it is age appropriate of course. Chances are, at some point as a parent, you are going to say or do something hurtful and sound like your narcissistic mother. As soon as you realize this, you need to apologize to your child immediately. You might as well use this as a teaching moment to, and explain why what you said or did was wrong. Also, you can teach your children about what kind of healthy boundaries they need to have and how to enforce them, how to recognize a narcissist and ways to deal with them. Narcissists really are everywhere, and children need to learn how to deal with them since chances are good they will be forced to at some point in their lives.

You also need to realize that as you heal, use wisdom regarding who you discuss this topic with. So many people blame victims, especially those who are victims of narcissistic abuse and invalidate their pain. This is not what you need as you heal, especially if you feel particularly sensitive at the time. I had a fascinating dream once on this very topic. In the dream, I saw my car sitting in a parking lot, probably about one hundred feet away. I was walking to my car when suddenly a little black sedan came out of nowhere and hit my car head on. I was livid! I love my car, and was ready to hurt whoever wanted to mess up my car. As I was running towards the scene, the sedan backed up and hit my car again. It did this several times. I noticed that my car was fine, did not even budge, but the sedan was totaled. The sedan's front end was getting shorter and shorter, as it was crushed in each time it hit my car. My car is a very big old car, basically a tank, so it should not have surprised me in the dream it survived the impact just fine. I stopped in my tracks, laughing, and amazed that someone would be so foolish as to total their own car while doing no damage to mine. I then woke from the dream, and God immediately showed me what it meant. I have tried explaining that I have C-PTSD, its symptoms, and some of my experiences to some people who frankly do not care. My hope was to make them understand it is awful to live with, and I cannot help the problems I have. God said for me not to be like that sedan. Forcing my thoughts on someone who does not care will hurt me more than them, like that sedan in my dream. Interestingly, He also showed me via that dream that other people can be like that black sedan, too. Some people insist on saying things like, "Your mother did the best she could. You should appreciate her more" and other similar, ridiculous comments when you tell them you were abused. Many people will force their opinions on you no matter how much you do not want to hear them or how wrong you know they are. They are so determined you will hear what they have to say, they will hurt themselves or make themselves look foolish if that is what it takes to make sure they are heard. When I have been in that situation, I remember that dream, and it really helps me to remember not to take their insensitivity personally. I hope it does you as well!

Many people also insist that if you are going to heal from narcissistic abuse that you need to get the narcissist out of your life. While this certainly makes sense and is very advisable in many situations, sometimes, it just is not possible for various reasons. I have had many emails from women who live with their narcissistic mother or spouse and cannot afford to move out, others who want to go no contact but do not feel strong enough to do so at the time, and still others who simply do not wish to take that drastic step. People who have gone no contact often have no sympathy for these people. They often believe that if no contact works for them, it should work for everyone. They criticize those still in relationship with a narcissist, saying things like they deserve what they get. They also fail to realize that if you are the child of a narcissist, severing ties with a parent is not an easy choice for everyone. In spite of the pain they cause, it still can be extremely hard to go no contact with your parent. I stopped speaking to my mother for six years, and the time leading up to that decision was incredibly difficult for me.

I wish to encourage you to ignore what others say. Going no contact with any narcissist is a big decision, especially if that person is a parent. You need to make the decision for yourself after much prayer and consideration. And remember - if you choose not go no contact, it does not make you weak or foolish. In fact, having the relationship teaches you a great deal and makes you stronger. My mother contacted me after six years of us not speaking, and after some prayer and consideration, I allowed her back into my life on a very limited basis. It has not been easy, but these last eight years with her have taught me a lot about ways to deal with her narcissism. I also have become very strong because I have had to be strong with her to survive. Some good has come from it that I could not have gained if we were still no contact.

There are alternatives for people in situations where no contact is not an option. To start with, I have learned to pray every time before dealing with my parents, asking God to give me whatever I need to deal with them such as strength, courage or wisdom.

Limited contact is invaluable when you have a narcissist in your life. It is what I have opted to do with my narcissistic parents. I deal with them only when I feel I am strong enough to do so. When I am not, I do not answer their phone calls or see them. If I am unsure, I pray as the phone is ringing, asking God if I should answer or not, then do as I feel He leads me to. As a result of me not being as available, they call and want to visit me less frequently. I believe this is because they realize I am providing less and less narcissistic supply.

Obviously, this solution is very hard to implement if you live with a narcissist, but do not lose hope. There are ways to cope with them as well. Asking logical, clear questions and expecting answers is one surprisingly effective tool in dealing with narcissists. Questions such as, "What exactly do you mean by that?" will throw a narcissist off her game, especially when you demand an answer. (By demand, I do not mean yelling or acting rude - calmly reminding her over and over if necessary that she has yet to answer your question is much more effective). Narcissists are so accustomed to getting their way without any confrontation, that when they finally are confronted, it baffles them.

Matter of factly calling the narcissist out on her behavior is also effective. Calmly stating things they have done may not get the narcissist to admit her wrongdoing, but it does make her aware that you know exactly what she is up to. For example, calmly saying, "Oh. So you weren't honest with me about that. Is there anything else I need to know about it?" while making sure she answers your question lets her know you are well aware of what she did and cannot get away with it. Yelling in anger about her lying to you only starts a fight where she is the victim and you are abusive/cruel/unreasonable/etc. This can be hard to do, I know, because you really want to wring her neck. However, I really urge you to try calm logic instead. I have had it work pretty well for me, which I think is about as good as can be expected when it comes to dealing with a narcissist. Later on, away from the narcissist, I vent my anger in my journal, pray or talk to a supportive friend.

Denying narcissistic supply is another effective tool in dealing with narcissists. Basically you do this by simply becoming boring. You do not provide information on your life (thus denying her of ammunition for insulting you later) and ignore her attempts to get complements and praise from you. Instead, accept the fact that you cannot discuss your life with this person and talk about her life or neutral topics instead. Keep your opinions to yourself, too, so she cannot tell you how wrong you are. Offer periodic, sincere complements if you feel the urge, but never praise her because she is hinting for it.

Also, never ever get lax with your boundaries! Always know what they are, and be prepared to enforce them firmly if need be. Since narcissists are well known for smashing through boundaries, you are going to need to enforce yours several times at least before the narcissist gets it. It may happen though so do not give up hope! It took me years of telling my mother to stop insulting my cats before she finally has learned if she does it, I am serious - I will kick her out of my home and never allow her to come back.

In conclusion of the topic of no contact, it is a very good option in many cases of a narcissistic relationship. The six years I had apart from my mother gave me time to learn and to heal, so when we did reconnect, I was better equipped to deal with her again. However, maintaining the relationship has its advantages too, such as helping you to grow stronger.

As you heal, your life will improve. You will gain more peace and joy, and if you are still dealing with a narcissist, the healthier ways you relate to her will mean less drama for you. However, healing can be scary. It changes your life. What was once normal is no longer acceptable. Your relationships change as you heal. You change as you heal as well, possibly even losing or gaining interests. The way you always coped no longer works for you, and you have to learn new ways. In a way, it is much like a part of you dies, that old, dysfunctional you. The good part though is that you are reborn into this beautiful, new, happy, healthy creation. Like the phoenix, you rise from the ashes of abuse into a beautiful new creation!

2 Corinthians 5:17 "Therefore if any man be in Christ, he is a new creature: old things are passed away; behold, all things are become new." (KJV)

Epilogue

Narcissistic abuse is so evil and insidious. It causes so much pain and suffering, which often can feel as if it is never ending. It is not something I would wish on my worst enemy. Since you have experienced it yourself, my heart truly goes out to you. My fervent prayer is that this book helps every single person who reads it.

I pray that after reading this book, you feel more capable to deal with the problems you have that have stemmed from narcissistic abuse, that you are more equipped now to deal with the issues you face.

I pray that you also gain creative and healthy ways to deal with your narcissist, provided that she or he is still a part of your life, especially if no contact is not an option for you.

I pray that if you are seriously considering going no contact, God will give you the strength to do so if it is the best solution for you, and the wisdom on how to handle it that brings you the least amount of narcissistic rage and retaliation.

I also pray that you take good care of yourself. Recovery is not an easy feat. It is a lot of hard, emotional work. I pray you never forget to take good care of yourself by taking frequent breaks and taking good care of your health.

I pray too that you celebrate yourself often. You made it! You survived one of the most horrific things a person can endure, narcissistic abuse, and with your sanity in tact! That is something of which you should be very proud!

You should be proud of yourself for another reason too. Many victims of narcissistic abuse become suicidal, often following through on their suicidal thoughts and ideation. You are still alive! You made it to the age you are now in spite of all of the pain! That is something to be very proud of, and I hope you are proud of that.

You also should celebrate the fact you had the insight to know something was wrong, and searched for answers. Not everyone does. Many people stay beaten down by the abuse, never looking for answers or ways to make healthy changes.

May God continue to bless your healing and your life!

Thank you for buying this book. I appreciate every single person who reads my books, and pray for you often.

With Love,
Cynthia

Index

abandonment 45, 116
absolute thinking 62, 63, 64
agoraphobia 55, 98
amygdala 98
ancient Greek mythology 2
anger .... ii, 6, 36, 37, 38, 39, 40, 41, 42, 43, 44, 53, 71, 75, 104, 114, 115, 117, 119, 120, 137
angry 47, 49
anti-depressants 33, 34, 35, 56
anxiety 29, 54, 55, 56, 57, 93, 95, 98, 102
attention 6, 10, 43, 44, 60, 65, 75, 79, 94, 107, 116, 117, 120, 126, 127, 133
balance 72, 73, 131
Bible .... iv, 2, 19, 34, 37, 38, 73

bizarre behavior	10
body language	11, 98
boundaries	8, 10, 22, 72, 77, 110, 127, 134, 137
breaking the silence	15
Briggs Myers Personality Test	28
bully	8
carbon monoxide poisoning	91, 102
celebrate your victories	133
chair technique	115
comfort	25, 29, 32, 33, 39, 41, 56, 58, 94, 112, 129
comfort zone	25, 29, 112
competitive	6
Complex Post Traumatic Stress Disorder/C-PTSD	iv, 13, 24, 25, 48. 64, 90, 91, 97, 98, 100, 101, 102, 103, 106, 108, 110, 117. 135
covert incest	10
covert narcissist	3, 5
cowards	8
crazymaking	31
creativity	34, 57, 65, 66, 67, 85, 139
criticism	7, 69, 79, 115, 126
criticize	6, 11, 15, 18, 20, 39, 62, 63, 65, 67, 94, 135
daughter in-law	6

demanding 6, 8, 75

depression 13, 31, 32, 33, 34, 38, 39, 87, 98, 110, 119, 131

desperate 43, 126, 127

dirty looks 11

dissociation 89, 90, 91, 99

Dissociative Identity Disorder/Multiple Personality Disorder ...90

dreams 106, 107, 108, 109, 133

emotional flashback 94, 96

emotional incest/parentification/parentalizing 10, 48, 76, 83

emotional regulation 97

empathy 8, 17, 103, 129

engulfing narcissistic mother 4, 54

entitled 5, 8, 131, 133

envious 6, 65

expectations 20, 67, 123

extension 10, 27, 61

fear 9, 14, 15, 55, 74, 95, 97, 100

feel guilty 15, 75, 123, 133

feeling robbed 47, 48, 49

femininity 34, 78, 79, 80, 81, 82

flashbacks 58, 93, 94, 95, 96, 99, 101

gaslighting/crazymaking 11, 17, 31, 69, 126

143

General Anxiety Disorder 55

God .... ii, iii, 2, 13, 15, 19, 20, 25, 26, 27, 33, 34, 37, 39, 43, 44, 45, 52, 53, 56, 57, 63, 70, 72, 73, 75, 80, 81, 84, 94, 103, 107, 109, 113, 115, 120, 124, 130, 133, 134, 136, 139, 140, 150

good things 19, 103, 129, 130, 133

grateful heart 129

grief 36

grounding 95

grow 8, 15, 138

heal .... i, iii, 13, 14, 26, 36, 37, 41, 44, 56, 64, 66, 90, 94, 104, 106, 111, 113, 120, 127, 128, 134, 135, 138

healthy 8, 13, 16, 18, 22, 23, 25, 36, 37, 39, 42, 52, 57, 62, 67, 72, 81, 91, 102, 103, 110, 112, 115, 127, 129, 133, 134, 138, 139, 140

hippocampus 98

hyper-vigilance 97, 98

hypocritical 9

identity 48

ignoring narcissistic mother 4, 5

inappropriate sexual behavior 10

INFJ 28

insecurity 4, 5, 6, 9, 66, 80, 132

144

intrusive thoughts 99

invalidate .... iii, 8, 15, 16, 48, 119, 120, 126, 129

It's All About ME! The Facts About Maternal Narcissism 12

Jesus 19, 44, 63, 122, 123

journal 16, 33, 39, 57, 115, 119, 137

judge 14, 15, 39

learn .... iii, 8, 13, 18, 20, 22, 27, 28, 29, 36, 41, 59, 71, 74, 88, 95, 104, 127, 128, 138

love 3, 7, 14, 18, 19, 33, 34, 44, 46, 57, 60, 67, 71, 83, 84, 85, 88, 103, 118, 121, 126, 127, 129, 130, 132, 133, 134

marrying a narcissist 125

martyrdom 4

megalomania 1

menstrual problems 80

mental illnesses 4

mirroring 11

mistakes 20, 39, 62, 63, 70, 127

mood swings 99

mother in-law 6

music 33

narcissistic abuse .... i, ii, iii, iv, 1, 11, 12, 13, 14, 15, 16, 17, 20, 21, 27, 29, 31, 37, 39, 41, 42, 43, 48, 51, 53, 59, 61, 64, 66, 67,

69, 72, 74, 75, 78, 83, 84, 90, 97, 102, 103, 104, 105, 106, 110, 111, 112, 114, 120, 121, 122, 123, 124, 126, 127, 129, 131, 133, 134, 135, 139, 140

narcissistic injury 7

narcissistic mother .... iv, 4, 6, 9, 10, 11, 16, 18, 28, 29, 36, 40, 42, 43, 54, 59, 60, 61, 64, 66, 69, 74, 78, 80, 119, 120, 125, 133, 134, 135

Narcissistic Personality Disorder .... i, iii, iv, 1, 2, 3, 4, 5, 7, 8, 13, 18, 19, 36, 59, 128, 132

narcissistic rage 7, 9, 11, 15, 54, 76, 110, 132, 139

narcissistic supply 132, 136, 137

Narcissus 2

National Suicide Prevention Hotline 32

negative 10, 25, 32, 51, 52, 53, 120, 122

nervous breakdown 74

nightmares 106, 108, 111

no contact 113, 121, 135, 136, 138, 139

Obsessive Compulsive Disorder 55

overt narcissist 3, 5

panic attacks 55, 98

personality 4, 28, 88, 90, 91

personality disorders 4

phobia	55
pray	63, 81, 107, 108, 112, 113, 119, 124, 136, 137, 139, 140
prefrontal cortex	97
prefrontal lobe	98
projection	9, 36, 53, 67, 132
prudish	10, 78
self-care	132
self-esteem	ii, 7, 11, 17, 18, 19, 20, 21, 22, 23, 27, 37, 41, 48, 52, 62, 66, 91, 99, 104, 114, 127, 132
selfish	ii, 3, 4, 16, 18, 31, 36, 114
self-sacrificing	4
service animal	57
sexual abuse/sexual assault	90
sexually inappropriate	10
shame	23, 24, 25, 26, 92, 94
shock	11, 59, 60, 61
silent treatment	7
social anxiety	55
spectrum disorder	4
St. John's Wort	56
strong	iii, 15, 33, 38, 78, 81, 82, 95, 102, 114, 130, 135, 136
suicide	32, 33, 39, 140

take breaks	13, 131
toxic shame	23, 24, 25, 26
triggers	93, 94, 99, 120, 123
unworthy	24
validating	16, 28, 33, 124
Why do narcisissts act the way they do	4
writing	iii, iv, 13, 15, 16, 33, 85, 88, 98, 107, 117, 150

About The Author

Cynthia Bailey-Rug is happily married to Eric Rug. Together they live outside Annapolis, Maryland with their menagerie of lovely pets. Cynthia has been a Christian since 1996, and believes God has called her to write. She always loved writing, but realized it was her purpose in 2003. She has since written many articles, started a successful blog and written several books. She enjoys animals, classic cars, yarn crafts, electronic gadgets.

Where To Find Cynthia Bailey-Rug Online

Website:
www.CynthiaBaileyRug.com

Facebook group:
https://www.facebook.com/groups/FansOfCynthiaBaileyRug/

Blog:
https://cynthiabaileyrug.wordpress.com/

Twitter:
https://twitter.com/CynthiaRug

Linkedin:
https://www.linkedin.com/in/cynthiabaileyrug

Tumblr:
http://www.tumblr.com/blog/cynthiabaileyrug

Google+:
https://plus.google.com/+CynthiaBaileyRug

Amazon:
http://amazon.com/author/cynthiabaileyrug

Smashwords:
https://www.smashwords.com/profile/view/CynthiaBaileyRug

Made in the USA
San Bernardino, CA
14 April 2017